Days of Healing, Days of Joy

The Hazelden Meditation Series

Twenty-Four Hours a Day
The Promise of a New Day: A Book of
    Daily Meditations
Each Day a New Beginning: Daily Meditations
    for Women
Today's Gift: Daily Meditations for Families
Night Light: A Book of Nighttime Meditations
Touchstones: A Book of Daily Meditations
    for Men
Day by Day: Meditations for Young Adults
Food for Thought: Daily Meditations for
    Dieters and Overeaters
The Love Book

Days of Healing, Days of Joy

Daily Meditations for Adult Children

by
Earnie Larsen
and
Carol Larsen Hegarty

Illustrations by
David Spohn

Harper/Hazelden

We would like to dedicate this book to Katie, Steve, and Bill — our brothers and sister — the tallest oaks in the forest, in our opinion, worthy pilgrims whom we dearly love.

Earnie Larsen   Carol Larsen Hegarty

INTRODUCTION

The thoughts shared in these brief readings are intended to assist adult children in their search for serenity. By provoking new insights, challenging accustomed viewpoints, and applauding small, but consistent efforts, we have attempted to convey the abiding sense of hope and help that characterizes all Twelve Step fellowships. As the grateful recipients of Twelve Step wisdom ourselves, we are obliged to do nothing less.

Recovery is a high-stakes proposition. Because the level of commitment required for this great journey is so great, a straightforward, sometimes blunt style has been used to present the ideas expressed here. Readers who do not relate to the tone or content of some of these meditations are encouraged to "take what you can use and leave the rest."

While it isn't possible to rewrite or obliterate the past, it is possible for each of us to reassess the building blocks of our own reality. With enough effort, direction, and help we can learn to move these building blocks around, push some out of the way, and add some new ones. The way it always has been doesn't mean that's the way it always will be.

As long as we are alive we have the power to polish, recut, and place the precious jewel of the self in a brand-new setting.

January

You are loved. If so, what else matters?
— Edna St. Vincent Millay

It is a critical task of recovery to get our priorities in order and keep them that way. Sometimes as we trudge the path of recovery, we find that our priorities have gotten out of whack. We can overextend ourselves in our efforts to learn to play, exercise, develop a prayer life, or acquire some of the material things that may have been missing from our lives for so many years.

As worthwhile as all of those efforts may be, they all work toward the same goal of helping us be people more capable of love. If we are truly loved and capable of functioning in loving relationships, what else really matters? What else is there? We may never have all the things we once thought were justly owed us, we may never be as able to play as we think we should, we may never know all we think we should know. But if we are able to glory in and share in the love around us, then we shall have found the key which makes life worth living.

What's important to me is changing. My wants are becoming fewer as I realize that my needs are already met.

January 2

Humility is to make a right estimate of oneself.
— *Charles Haddon Spurgeon*

What does it take to come to the place where we can exchange pride for humility? First we must stop the blasphemous charade of pretending that we are no good. "I'm worthless" has often been spoken in the name of humility. But these words, or any other words that express the same sentiment, are a self-indulgence and a cop-out.

The essence of humility is summed up in the Serenity Prayer: God grant me the serenity to accept the things I cannot change, courage to change the things I can, and wisdom to know the difference.

Humility is truth. To be humble is to know the truth about our limits, to recognize what can be changed, and to accept that all good things are possible with the help of our Higher Power.

Excessive pride prohibits acceptance because it prohibits the truth, and the truth is that some things are unchangeable. Refusal to accept that truth gets us plenty of frustration and anger — and no humility at all.

Today, I humbly ask God for the wisdom to accept what is and to let go of what isn't.

Talk doesn't cook rice.
> — *Chinese Proverb*

Some of us are crazy about self-help books, inspirational tapes, and personal improvement seminars. We'll buy or sign up for anything, whatever the price, if it promises revolutionary insights or a foolproof new system. We want relief in a day and deliverance in a weekend. And we want the expert of the hour to do it for us.

There's nothing wrong with wishing, of course. But there's a lot wrong with kidding ourselves as a way of life. Think about it: If progress could be bought, we wouldn't need to be meditating. If personal transformation resulted from collecting new ideas, we'd have been transformed long ago. Exploring is great. And looking for all the inspiration and wisdom we can find is necessary for growth. But changing is doing. All the plans and schemes for improvement put together won't change a thing if we don't put the principles into daily practice. Even catchy words are just words.

Today, I will take the best plan I have and put it into action. Today, I will say less and do more.

January 4

Without work all life goes rotten.
— Albert Camus

Most would not think of work as a prize. That is often due to the concept we have of work.

Work can be that of an artist, the work of creation. Such work is not the response to a whistle or the boring activity that follows a punched time card. Creative work is the fullest human expression of being alive. It comes from the inside out and has no boss other than an inner demand to create a thing of beauty that previously did not exist.

The primary task of human beings is to creatively work at making their lives a remarkable thing of beauty. Whether we be butcher, baker, or candlestick maker there is always the opportunity to make a truly creative effort of a life's work by pounding out our dents and polishing that which is already beautiful. When we understand that life is the medium and we are the canvas, our efforts to improve become an exciting challenge rather than a boring task.

I am grateful to have the opportunity and the strength to work. I will not resent my job.

God hasn't called me to be successful.
He's called me to be faithful.
— *Mother Teresa*

A reporter asked Mother Teresa how she could bear to go on working at such a hopeless task day after day and year after year. The people she cares for are so wretchedly poor. Many of them are very sick. How could she continue with such dedication, knowing that all the poverty and sickness will still be there long after she's dead? Didn't she realize she couldn't win?

Her explanation is simple: Of course she knows the task is immense, but "finishing" isn't her purpose. Mother Teresa has turned her life and will over to God, and her work is what she believes to be God's will for her. Because of this, she is devoted to the task itself, not to the completion of it.

We too can learn to be receptive to a higher purpose. We can direct our energies into causes we believe in, even if we know the job will never be finished. We can visit with friends and family and not try to win a verbal exchange. We can accept the will of our Higher Power and thereby find serenity.

Today, I will let go of the driving need to succeed or to impress others. Instead, I will be receptive to my Higher Power's will.

January 6

> *At bottom every man knows well enough that he is a unique human being, only once on this earth; and by no extraordinary chance will such a marvelously picturesque piece of diversity in unity as he is, ever be put together a second time.*
>
> — *Nietzche*

Each of us is a one-and-only. No one sees the world just as we do. No one has our laugh or smile, our exact way of walking and talking. Besides our handwriting and our fingerprints, we are unique in a hundred other ways; our thinking style, our sense of humor, our tastes have never come together in one person before, and they never will again. We are truly ourselves and no one else, matched to our place and time in history and no other.

We are related to, but not defined by, those who came before us. Their choices need not be our choices, their mistakes and limits need not be ours. They are different people matched to a different time. We are not who they are and we are not responsible for who they are. We are new people and this is a new day. *Our* day. No one else can live this life for us. Let us go forward.

Today, I pray for the wisdom to see myself as the precious, unequaled human being that I am. Let me be aware that the life I've been given is mine.

*Psychotics think two and two make
five. Neurotics know two and two
make four — but they can't stand it.*
        — Anonymous

We cook up a good batch of frustration when
we insist on having it both ways. But, whether we
like it or not, every yes is also a no. A yes to
playing with money is a no to a nest egg. A yes to
the late movie is a no to an energetic morning. As
the proverb says, "You can't make the bed and save
the sheet."

It's a good idea to check out our priorities before
we punish ourselves with the yes-no game. While
we can't have it both ways, we can have peace of
mind if we think through the trade-off before we
make it. Sometimes we'll find we've been torturing
ourselves unnecessarily — if a piece of cherry pie
really gives us more pleasure than a smaller waist-
line — we should admit it, accept it, and enjoy the
pie without guilt. What is worse is losing both
ways: making our choices and then denying ourselves the pleasure of those choices by giving in to
guilt. Life is too short to waste energy on phony
dilemmas. Let's give ourselves a break.

*Today, I will try to give full assent to the choices I
make. Fence-sitting is an uncomfortable habit.*

January 8

May you live all the days of your life.
— Jonathan Swift

Indeed life is much like a game — both a deadly serious one and one that demands laughter, relaxation, and the ability to play. Either way, life demands attention.

There is much of life that is truly exciting and fascinating — are we watching for it? There is hilarity and humor — do we see it? There is that in life which is touching and full of heroism — are we open to seeing it?

All these are not only present in some general, nebulous way about life, but about our lives! Right here where we live, in our lives today, there will be the hero and the goat, there will be disappointment and reason for wild celebration, there will be the beautiful and the horrible. The soap opera is not out there; it is right here with us, in us, all around us. The task is to be present in our own lives, to get our heads out of others' reality, and to find the enormous meaning and vitality of our own.

Life is precious. Today, I will not take my life for granted.

A life without discipline is a life without joy.

> — *Muriel B.*

Wait a minute. Isn't joy a matter of doing what we want? Isn't freedom the state of never having to do what we don't want to do? And isn't discipline — which we learned from our parents — the burden of having to do what we don't want to do?

Actually, joy is the freedom to do what needs to be done. And gaining that freedom takes discipline. Why? Without discipline, we usually ended up doing what is familiar to us. And our experience clearly tells us that old thinking and old behaviors bring us anything but joy.

It takes discipline to say no when we need to — when every fiber of our being may be urging us to give in again. It takes discipline to stand up and be counted when our pattern has been to fade into the wallpaper and blend in with any situation.

Discipline isn't easy or fun, but it's the best friend we can have. To practice self-discipline is to move through our days with a sure sense that we'll get where we're going.

Today, I will remember that self-discipline is in my self-interest.

January 10

'Tis peace of mind, lad, we must find.
— Theocritus

What could be more valuable than peace of mind? With it, no other valuables are necessary. Without it, all the valuables in the world aren't enough. Truly, no human condition is more desirable.

All languages have words for the profound sense of serenity that is peace of mind. Liberians talk about peace of mind in words that literally mean, "My heart sits down." In other parts of Africa, peace of mind is called a "body song" or "where the cool water runs." In any tongue, the sentiment is the same.

Peace of mind isn't something we go out and get. It's the result of something we do and keep on doing. Peace is the reward for turning our lives and our wills over to the care of God as we understand Him, so we can do what is necessary. When our response to shame is not a food binge, the afterglow is peace of mind; when we want to run from a relationship but don't, we have earned the sensation of peace; when we want to hide but we extend a heart and hand, we have won peace.

Today, I will prepare myself to receive peace of mind. I will thank God in advance for giving it to me.

*Anger helps straighten out a problem
like a fan helps straighten out a pile of
papers.*

— *Susan Marcotte*

Some of us have temper tantrums. Like black clouds, we threaten an outburst at any moment. Other people learn to check us out for storm warnings. They want time to clear out or at least to put on a protective covering. We've caught them by surprise before, and they didn't like it. Now they've learned to watch out — to stay on their toes when we're around. Intimidating people, making them glad when we're not around so they can relax is a poor way to relate to others.

And what do the outbursts do for us? Is there a cheap sense of power or control for a few minutes? Are we advertising to the world that we're short on coping skills? Or do we tell ourselves that letting off steam is necessary once in a while, conveniently forgetting the steam blasting in other people's faces?

No tirade ever solved a problem. Anger is not a strategy. We don't have the right to rain on other people's parades. Our program can teach us better ways to deal with our anger — with honesty and fairness to ourselves and others.

Today, I ask my Higher Power for a peaceful and honest heart.

January 12

> *What I* said *never changed anybody;*
> *what they* understood *did.*
>
> — *Paul P.*

How often have we given our all to change somebody else? How frantically have we tried to force a loved one to see the light? How hopelessly have we watched a destructive pattern — perhaps a pattern we know well from personal experience — bring terrible pain to someone who is dear to us?

All of us have.

We would do anything to save the people we love. In our desperation, we imagine that if we say just the right words in just the right way, our loved ones will understand.

If change happens, we think our efforts have succeeded.

If change doesn't happen, we think our efforts have failed. But neither is true. Even our best efforts don't have the power to change someone else. Nor do we have that responsibility. People are only persuaded by what they understand. And they, as we, can understand a deeper truth only when it is their time to grow toward deeper understanding. Not before.

Today, I will focus on changing myself and entrust those I love to the Higher Power who loves them even more than I do.

God will wait as long as it takes for us.
— *Rev. R. Walters*

Whenever we try to understand, analyze, or probe too much into the reasons for love, we damage it. All that can really be done with love is accept it.

God has said He loves us. We are loved. Regardless of all the painful experiences we may have had that convinced us love never lasts, or that love may be fine for others but it just doesn't work for us — regardless of what we may have learned of love — God has said He loves us.

There is a lovely parable in Scripture about the lost sheep and the steadfast love of the shepherd. When the one sheep became lost, as the parable goes, the shepherd did not simply write it off as the cost of doing business. The shepherd searched diligently until the lost sheep was found. No mention is made of scolding, abuse, or punishment — simply the joy the shepherd felt at finding one of his own that was lost.

We are as loved as that lost sheep; and, at times, as lost. Whether we feel we are worth it or not, the Shepherd patiently, faithfully searches us out. We cannot outrun God's reach.

Today, I ask God to deepen my faith.

January 14

Defeat may serve as well as victory
To shake the soul and let the glory out.
— Edwin Markham

So life has given us some dents. So what? Dents are necessary, besides being unavoidable and painful. Each dent is a part of the process that enables us to embrace life as a creative experience and to see the world in a new way, a way of compassion and understanding. Recovery is not a matter of escaping further blows or of disguising the dents we already have. It's a matter of understanding what the dents mean and how we can work with them.

Dents are neither soft spots in our characters that should make us ashamed nor saber scars that should make us proud. They are simply evidence that we have been alive for a while. Recovery offers us the chance to learn from our dents, to accept them as new spaces for growth. When we decide to see our dents as opportunities gained rather than opportunities lost, we stand much taller in our own eyes and in the eyes of others.

Today, I will look on my difficult life experiences in a new light. Today, I will plant some seeds.

Nice guys finish last.
> — Leo Durocher

Some of us are habitually victims, doormats, "poor things." No matter what, we never say no. The more we practice being nice guys the less able we are to cope creatively. We place the blame, along with the responsibility, elsewhere.

Darlene modeled this for all of us at a recent meeting. She is well past fifty and has been divorced for twenty years. Yet she is still seeking sympathy for what her husband — and God — did to her. Twenty-five years ago she inherited fifty thousand dollars from her parents' estate. Bit by bit, as she said, her alcoholic husband spent it all. It wasn't that she gave it to him or failed to manage it herself, she explained. What happened was that he "just spent it all up. How could he do that?" The obvious, healthier question never occurred to her: How could she allow a sick person to eat up a small fortune?

The moral of the story is that being "too nice" isn't our problem.

Today, I will search my conscience for evidences of irresponsibility that I may have been filing under other names.

January 16

Inches make champions.
— Vince Lombardi

What's the difference between success and failure? Ideal conditions? Half again as much effort? Twice the talent? Ten times "the breaks"? Or is it simply that some people have what it takes and some people don't?

Vince Lombardi, the football coach who brought the Green Bay Packers from fifteen losing seasons to successive world championships, thought success was a matter of inches. A bit more concentration, one extra push in practice, a consistent second effort for a tiny additional gain. He didn't ask his players to be something other than they were — he asked them to improve their best an inch at a time. He knew inches add up, in life as in sports.

In life as in football, it is often the little things that count: going to meetings when we feel like staying home, or speaking our minds, no matter how insignificant our opinion may seem. When we feel like simply hiding — inches make the difference.

Today, I will be aware that I am a champion in the making. I may not make a complete turnaround today, but I will make progress.

Now that I'm not acting crazy I can
accept feeling crazy once in a while.
                                    — Sandy B.

Saying no to ourselves may be a greater act of courage than rushing into a burning building to save a child. The act of heroic rescue may be impulsive, almost involuntary, and completed before there is time for a reasoned judgment. Ah, but the other one! To consciously challenge our own will is never a spontaneous thing. We may feel crazy the first day we deny ourselves the familiar comfort of nicotine or other substances. The first, or fifth, or twenty-fifth time we practice detachment may make us feel like we're coming apart. First efforts at taking responsibility for our own behavior can make us feel as peculiar and disjointed as if we'd decided to go through the rest of our lives walking on our hands instead of our feet.

But to be crazy is to keep on asking for what we don't want. If, for a while, sane action has to be accompanied by crazy feelings — then so be it. To accept that paradox and forge ahead anyway is to join the ranks of heroes who don't get medals. No medal can adequately symbolize those fierce and private battles.

Today, I ask my Higher Power for a surer sense of mission.

January 18

> *He has served who now and then*
> *Has helped along his fellowmen.*
> — *Edgar A. Guest*

It's hard to be interested in something that seems too remote. Sure, we're sorry for starving people in faraway places. And the TV news story about whole villages disappearing in an earthquake makes us feel terrible — until the next news story comes on. It doesn't mean we're bad people when we don't respond much to such tragedies. It only means they're not personal — and only the personal is real.

We care most about what we're involved in directly. If we're not personally involved, we're not very enthusiastic either. If we are the ones starting a new ACOA meeting, setting up the chairs, making the coffee, the success of that meeting means a lot to us. If our children are on drugs, we're not bored by city council meetings where new drug programs are discussed. It's our stake in something that makes it important.

The world doesn't need any more spectators. To feel more alive, we must be more alive. Caring is life and involvement is growth.

Today, I will not sit on the sidelines. I will act on behalf of a good cause that deserves my support.

Because I have been athirst
I will dig a well that others may drink.
— *Arabian Proverb*

Most of us do as we please. When we want to go, we go; when we want to stay, we stay. We're accustomed to moving around freely and never even think about it. We trust that a door will open if we turn the knob and push. Unfortunately, we never appreciate what we take for granted, and we are less for that.

A young man at an adult child meeting shared that he had just been released from prison, where doors are locked. Upon release, the first thing he had done, he said, was to walk back and forth across the pressure plate of the bus station door. *He* wanted to be the one to make a door open and close. Onlookers had laughed at him, he said, but he didn't care. He appreciated the chance to move, to go where he wanted. Having known the hell of doors that won't open, he had an awareness that the rest of us didn't have. As his recovery continues, he will have much to share with people who've been trapped in prisons of their own.

May I have the insight to recognize my own special qualifications, and the willingness to share them with others.

January 20

The program has given me the best days I've ever had. But thinking about all that lost time can still bring me down.

— Jane S.

Telling the difference between yesterday, today, and tomorrow may be easy for most people, but it isn't for many of us. Our past tends to overshadow both the present and the future. Until we learn to draw a line between then and now, the gloom of "what was" expands and spreads like noxious smoke or a sickening odor. "What can be" is blotted out.

Where does yesterday end and today begin? For us, that may be the central recovery issue. Our battle is one of boundaries.

No matter how spoiled the past may have been, our future is spotless. If, in our minds, we say good-bye to the past, we can begin writing a new story and painting a new picture.

Every day is new — fresh and shimmering with possibilities. The future is a long string of such days. As our perception of time corrects itself, as we learn to accept the past and look forward to the future, we can focus on today and live it well.

Today, I will see the bad days of the past as rotten apples. I will throw them out of my barrel to protect my new days.

*Resolve to be thyself; and know that
who finds himself, loses his misery.*
— *Matthew Arnold*

Our need for approval compels us to try to look
good — no matter what's going on. We imagine
that somehow everything will be okay as long as it
looks okay. Our hearts may be breaking from fear,
disillusionment, and rejection, real or imagined,
but we keep smiling so that no one will guess. Why
do we do this to ourselves? Is it so hard to turn to a
friend and say, "Hey, I'm hurting. I've been having
a bad time and I need help"? Would the earth trem-
ble if we said it right out, just like that?

We're not likely to get what we don't ask for.
Instead of denying that our knees are shaking, our
hands are sweating, and our stomachs are in tor-
ment, we can admit and share the truth. We don't
have to say "Fine!" when someone in the program
asks us how we're doing. Our real friends aren't
impressed by stiff upper lips; they're impressed by
personal honesty.

*Today, I will tell someone the truth about how I
feel. If I'm not fine I won't say that I am.*

> *Hope and patience are two sovereign*
> *remedies for all, the surest reposals, the*
> *softest cushions to lean on in adversity.*
> — *Robert Burton*

It is just as easy to think "I can" as it is to think "I can't." Both attitudes are habitual orientations to life that can become automatic with practice. Neither attitude has as much to do with the task at hand as it does with the inner spirit of the person facing the task. In either case, the task is the same — only the attitude is different.

But what a difference! The "I can" people are the ones we want to spend time with and to use as models. These are the people who either have never lost, or have worked to regain the positive outlook we are all born with. It never occurs to a baby, for example, that all that staggering and falling means he or she will never learn to walk. Babies grow, move forward, succeed. They haven't learned to hang back or fear defeat. Knee-jerk negativity is something we can all do without. Let's backtrack to that time in our lives when all things were possible . . . because they still are.

Today, I will focus on my successes. "I can" is my
credo.

At 70, my dad is just like he was at 35
— only more so. It's frightening that
the same thing could happen to me.
— Jerry Z.

More of the same gets more of the same. What
we were given to practice, we practiced. What we
practiced, we became. What we became, we are
continuing to become — only more so — every
day of our lives. We can do ourselves a favor by
being aware of what we practice. Has the past
taught us to withdraw? Think of how isolated we'll
be twenty years from now! Have we practiced generalized distrust? Imagine how deep the roots of
fear are growing.

But there's another side to that truth. If we practice finding beauty today, we'll find twice as much
beauty tomorrow. If we work on forgiveness today, tomorrow we may be free of resentments. If
we choose to relate rather than isolate, we can
walk with friends through all the years that stretch
before us. What will the future bring us? Whatever
we have invested in it.

I pray for the wisdom to see my future as largely
the work of my own hands and heart. I pray for
the courage to take responsibility for choosing my
own direction.

The purpose of learning is growth, and our minds, unlike our bodies, can continue growing as we continue to live.
— *Mortimer Adler*

In some areas of our lives we are right on target. Our level of maturity is exactly as it should be, and we are going through the stages that people of our age ought to be going through. In other areas, this is not so. We are complex people, irregular, uneven. In all of us there are areas fixated in some emotional ice age, areas that have not felt the freeing warmth of the sun.

We cannot expect ourselves to move forward all at once. Not only is it okay to move slowly — it's often the only way it can be. Confusion, conflict, or pain may have caused us to let our memories or feelings be frozen safely away. This has been a long process, and we can allow ourselves more time to heal. The task now is not to deny or hide from these changes, but to have confidence that the healing warmth of the program will reflect on all areas of our lives and help make us whole.

I am thankful I am given both time and patience in which to continue my growth.

Only those means of security are good,
are certain, are lasting, that depend on
yourself and your own vigor.
— *Machiavelli*

What is our security based upon? This is a vital, bottom-line question.

Security is a basic need of all humans. But as with all quests, if we look for the object of our search in an area where it cannot be found, we court certain frustration and failure.

Many would base their security on outside conditions. That is building our house on sand. Beauty passes, fame is fleeting, wealth can quickly evaporate, and health is fragile at best. What then is safe to count upon?

Only one security cannot be taken away, and it resides within. Security based on our own belief in ourselves, in our ability not only to cope and survive, but to celebrate life is the only security that lasts. As hard as it may be for adult children to learn they can trust themselves, it still is the only lasting security.

My security rests on the gains I've made in the program. I've never had a stronger sense of self.

> *I find it awfully hard to give myself a
> break. I don't know where that attitude
> comes from.*
>
> — *Walker I.*

"I can't. I shouldn't. It's my fault." These self-abasing and self-defeating thoughts are expressions of shame. Because repeated thoughts turn into beliefs and long-held beliefs turn into actions, thoughts rooted in shame can lead to tragedy.

People who live in shame come to believe that it is not okay to make a mistake. They imagine they should know what to do without having to learn it. They think their wrong judgments mean they themselves are wrong.

But it is human to make mistakes. If we acknowledge we are human, we are defining ourselves as people who always have something to learn (Thomas Edison failed to perfect the light bulb until his ten-thousandth try). We are saying we have to keep going if our plans don't work out right away (Walt Disney went bankrupt seven times before he met with success).

"Thou shalt not be human" is the command of shame. What rubbish! How can we be anything else? Why would we want to be?

I pray I will live comfortably with human limitations. I will try to accept from myself what I accept from others.

*Take the matter of being born. What
does being born mean to most people?*
— *e. e. cummings*

Somewhere in this meditation book each of us
will find our birthday. It may cause us panic and
trauma. It may be a day that reminds us we are
getting older. For many adult children it causes
sadness because it reminds them of their childhood
birthdays.

Whatever that special day has meant to us in the
past, we are in control of what it can mean now
and in the future.

A birthday, like any yearly holiday, is a symbol,
a time to reflect and remember a special meaning.
The special meaning of birthdays can become a
reminder that we are called on to be reborn regularly. Seeing new beauty is a kind of rebirth. Making a decision, no matter how small, that enhances
our life is a form of rebirth. Moving on to a new
place, a new state of freedom, is being born again.
Every day can be a birthday.

*Today, I am celebrating the birth of a wholly wor-
thy human being. Any day I choose can be another birthday.*

January 28

*You love me so much, you want to put
me in your pocket. And I should die
there smothered.*
— D. H. Lawrence

Adult children often try to control people to
keep them from moving away. To assure that we
won't be left alone, we might smother-love them
with everything we have.

Of course we become obsessed with the person
we're trying to control. But even worse, this care-
taking behavior eventually leads us to become
more addicted to the problem than to the person.
We become good at solving other people's problems and wiping away their tears; that's our skill.
And that's why we so often end up attracting and
being attracted to people who have monumental
personal problems.

Oftentimes, our very hanging on guarantees the
relationship will fail. When we try to control those
we love we stand the chance of crippling ourselves
and our loved ones. We must first aim for being
healthy ourselves — only then can we learn to be
part of a healthy relationship.

*Today, I will let my loved ones face their own
problems. I can love these people without fixing
them.*

We admitted we were powerless over alcohol — that our lives had become unmanageable.
— Step One of Alcoholics Anonymous

Accepting powerlessness is a prerequisite of recovery. As adult children, the very idea may seem puzzling or even laughable. Haven't we felt powerless all along? Shouldn't we be trying to move away from powerlessness and toward power?

But in the program we've found powerless to have a different meaning. We see how we have exhausted all the nonproductive, ineffective ways to deal with our situation. Powerlessness here means we're giving up on willpower, force, and intellectualizing because they just didn't work.

When we admit we are powerless we are saying that we are through trying to do it on our own — finished with attempts at recovery which are centered around our own strength or cunning. To lay down our old failed powers is not much different, after all, from laying down a broken old bike with two flat tires. It was better than nothing, but now we have a new means of moving on our way.

Today, I am relieved and grateful to unburden myself of unrealistic expectations.

January 30

As the twig is bent the tree inclines.
— *Virgil*

A positive self-image is critical to our recovery. Why? Because it is the glasses through which we look, the gloves with which we touch, the door by which we enter into a relationship with life. Self-image is not who we really are, but a combination of who we wish we were, who we're afraid we are, and who we imagine other people think we are.

We act out in detail the role we've assigned ourselves in this world. That role, our self-image, works like a key that either fits or doesn't fit a world full of locked doors. Different keys open different doors. And some doors lead to bad places, as we all know. It isn't easy to change keys, but it is infinitely worth it. One reason is that we always pass our self-image on to our children; they know us too well to be fooled. If we want our children to walk tall, laugh happily, and sing joyously — we ourselves must do these things for them to see.

Today, I pray for the courage to challenge my tendency to discount myself. All my strong points will be very clear to me today.

*At first I resented it when my friends in
the program told me to be God or let
God.*

— *Myrna K.*

Who consciously decides to play God? Not me.
Not you. But many of us have a terrible time letting God run the world. No matter how much we
resolve not to, we take responsibility for things we
can't control. That's what playing God is, and
that's what a lot of us have practiced for a long,
long time. Playing God is not only hard work; it's
also a good way to ruin relationships. People just
don't like to be around would-be, mortal "gods"
whose clay feet are all too visible. Our good intentions don't make people feel less defensive about
us.

Letting go isn't easy. Especially if we confuse
letting go with not caring. Of course we care. But
that does not and must not mean we are responsible. Can we care enough to let others make their
own mistakes, earn their own victories, and take
responsibility for their own lives? Not to do so, no
matter how we may feel about it, breeds dependency in both them and us.

We must care enough to let them be.

*Today, I will be aware that "doing for" someone
else is also "doing to" him or her.*

February

When I grow up, I want to be a child.
— Dick H.

Some of us adult children need to grow up before we can be the children we never were. It may take years to grow old and wise enough to be young, but it's possible. With enough insight, determination, and change we can regain our lost childhood.

What does it take to do that? First, it takes a decision, and then it takes the willingness to build the necessary skills. How much is it worth to reclaim that childhood? Is it worth everything? That's how much commitment needs to be behind the decision. No wistful "wouldn't it be wonderful if" will do it.

What are the skills of a child? Openness, lightheartedness, trust, the ability to expect wonderful surprises. Those of us who didn't learn these attitudes effortlessly and naturally will have to practice. But if we choose to, we can learn. We can learn to build sand castles, to wonder about mysterious possibilities, and to expect the good in each new day. The world surrounding little children is the same world surrounding us. The viewpoint is the crucial difference. For us, a merry heart is a matter of choice.

Today, I will pray for young eyes and a young heart.

February 2

> *People are always blaming their circumstances for being what they are. The people who get on in this world are the people who get up and look for the circumstances they want, and if they can't find them, make them.*
> — *George Bernard Shaw*

If only the weather were better, people were friendlier, there were more job opportunities, less traffic, the family lived nearer, the taxes were lower, and the morning sun didn't shine on the wrong side of the house . . . we'd probably be happy right where we are. The problem is there's too much pressure here, too many frustrations and irritations. The answer seems simple enough — move to another house or city, or even another country.

The problem is that when we move, we take ourselves along. Where we are is where we have chosen to be. If we don't "fix our chooser," we'll choose the same people and predicaments again and again.

There is enormous freedom in accepting this truth. When we do, we claim the power to control the quality of our own lives and to create our own destiny.

Today, I will investigate how my choices have shaped my life.

Why do I feel so lonely all the time? I just can't figure it out.
— *LaVonne D.*

Loneliness is part of the human condition, and it really doesn't have a lot to do with whether we're around other people or not. Many of us have, at times, felt lonely in a crowd.

The essence of loneliness is isolation from self. As we learn to know and comfortably accept ourselves, silence can become a friend. Those who have grown to this level of self-acceptance are never truly alone.

There is a rub, of course. For years we may not have wanted our own company because we haven't liked ourselves. We haven't been willing to peek beyond the walls of our most private and personal secrets. And why? Were we afraid nothing would be there but damage and disappointment?

But the program shows us that it isn't true. There is not damage, disappointment, and failure at our core. What is there is a beautiful person doing the best possible with the tools at hand.

As we go on, we need never be lonely as we once were.

Today is "gratitude day." Today, I am thankful for my growth.

February 4

Ah, surely nothing dies but something mourns.
— *George Gordon (Lord Byron)*

Grief swoops down on us when we have lost something of value — like a good job or a dear friend. While the grieving process is painful, most of us recognize that it is normal, natural, and that it won't last forever. It's harder to understand the grief that recovery sometimes causes. Are we not leaving behind that which has no positive value? Why should we be sad? Are we doing something wrong?

But our old habits and patterns have been like valuable friends. They helped us cope when nothing else did. Even though we now see our old ways as tricks and scams, they have protected us for many years. They made us feel safe even when we weren't.

Destructive though they proved to be, the old ways were comfortable while they lasted. Naturally, there's a sense of grief when we leave them behind, just as a fresh cut naturally bleeds for a while — before it starts healing.

I understand and accept my momentary feelings of loss.

I am not responsible for my feelings —
only for what I do with them.
      — *Dr. Ceophus Martin*

Most feelings are unbidden, mysterious, and nebulous. We don't make a deliberate decision to call up one feeling or another. Feelings simply crop up into consciousness without our permission.

For no apparent reason, we may again feel the paralyzing fear of abandonment or a terrifying sense of isolation. Such emotions may come on us with the power to make us feel invisible in a world of real people and things.

The most trivial word, image, or even smell can activate the deeply hidden triggers of our feelings. We can't control the triggers, but we can control what we do with our feelings. Emotional management is learned, not inborn. Positive action is, was, and always will be the best remedy for wayward feelings. And consistent, positive action is the very definition of competent emotional management.

Now that I'm learning to act instead of react, bursts of negative feeling give me less trouble than they once did.

February 6

Guilt has very quick ears to an accusation.

— Henry Fielding

A fellow at a meeting told a strange story to make a point about the very human tendency to take on undeserved guilt. The story was about a little trick he liked to play in his office once in a while. It seems he would choose a fellow employee at random, approach him innocently, and whisper, "They know," while looking around furtively. Then he would walk away quickly and watch what happened from a distance. Inevitably, he said, the recipient of this strange message first looked bewildered and then looked worried. Sometimes the person would start to sweat, the man said, and every time his frantic thoughts became nearly visible on his face: "Oh my God, how much do they know? What will they do about it? Will they tell anyone?"

The point was that nearly everybody is vulnerable to shame. Even the innocent have a knee-jerk tendency to conceal and protect. How horrified would we be, he asked, if someone whispered "They know" to us? Would we panic? Or would we be healthy enough to laugh it off since there is nothing anyone else could know that we aren't already dealing with?

Today, I pray for the courage to keep on working through my fear.

It ain't over 'til it's over.

— *Yogi Berra*

An outside observer might look at us adult children and shake his head in disbelief. Grown-up people struggling with such basic tasks and asking such basic questions! Who am I? What do I feel? How do I fit? What really happened to me? What can I do about it? Who might help me? How can I trust them? How can I trust myself? On the face of it, our aspirations do seem fairly improbable. The job is too big and the timing is too far off. The odds, the observer might conclude, are against us.

But starts aren't finishes, we might explain to the observer. Many a likely prospect has proved a disappointment and many a dark horse has come surging out of the pack to the great surprise of the odds-players. People are too complex, human dynamics are too mysterious, to judge by mathematical predictions. Desire and determination can mock the odds every time. We have decided to make our own odds; we invite observers to watch what happens.

Today, I pray for the courage to persist in spite of discouragement. I will not forget that I was born to win.

February 8

Growth is the only evidence of life.
— *Cardinal Newman*

There's a great temptation in our materialistic society to hire people to solve our problems. Want to get rid of the snow on the sidewalk? Hire a kid with a shovel. "Here's the problem," we say to our lawyers, counselors, and politicians, "Make it go away." Thus the assumption grows that *any* problem, and the responsibility for solution, can and should be handed off to someone else.

Yet some problems just can't be hired out — no matter how inadequate we feel about solving them ourselves and no matter how much money we have to buy help. The need for personal renewal is one such problem. No one else can rescue us from ourselves. No "expert" could possibly know as much as we do about where we've been and what we need to go on. Our own personal growth is our own personal responsibility. Either we take on the job or we don't — it's as simple, and as difficult, as that.

I will face a problem I've been avoiding. Dealing with it won't be as painful as fearing it.

*When all is said and done, willingness
is everything.*
                                            — Frank D.

Most of us adult children know very well that
recovery doesn't happen, nor is there any positive
growth, unless we are first of all willing.

Sometimes we get confused over the difference
between willing and wanting. We don't have to
want, let alone enjoy, doing what needs to be
done. Not wanting to do something is altogether
different from not being willing to do it. As one
recovering woman said, "Everything I ever let go
of had claw marks all over it." The bottom line is
that she did let go no matter how badly she wanted
to hang on: she was willing.

Think of the people in the program we most
admire, those whose progress seems so speedy
compared to ours. They may very well not enjoy
going out to meetings. They may find it uncomfortable to meet with their sponsors or to say kind
words when they really want to complain. They
may wish they didn't have to make amends to certain people. But druthers aren't the point. The
point is that they are willing to do what it takes.

*Today, I ask God to help me deepen my willing-
ness to grow and to see the difference between
what I want and what I will.*

February 10

Stronger by weakness, wiser men become.

— *Edmund Waller*

There is a good bit of truth in the old saying, "Tell me your strengths, and I'll tell you your weaknesses." Every plus has its flip side. Efficient people, for example, may tend to be so organized that they can come up with an answer before they hear the question. In the program, these sturdy souls often set about fixing their character flaws quickly. Then, just as quickly, frustration sets in. Their quick-fix problem-solving techniques always worked before. Why should this be different?

Highly intelligent people may tend to be arrogant and impatient. All their lives they have wondered why others are so slow to catch on. But when recovery calls for wisdom instead of intelligence, they're beside themselves with irritation. They've gotten A's all their lives, so why can't they figure this one out? How can it be that smart isn't right?

Most of us think of our strong points as our treasures. It may be we would learn something if we check out the other side of the coin.

In taking my inventory today, I'll check to make sure I've correctly labeled my strengths and character defects.

And behold you were within me,
and I out of myself,
and there I searched for you.
                    — *St. Augustine*

Augustine, remember, was the man who asked God to give him chastity — but not yet. He was one of the original buy-now-and-pay-later thinkers. Many of us can identify with the dilemma that gripped Augustine for so many years: We know that our wrongs are many and grievous. We know what we need to do, and we certainly intend to do it — soon, but not quite yet.

One of these days, right? When Augustine finally got around to giving up his delusion and denial, he became one of the towering figures of his century. But what of us? Will we outlast our willfulness? Or will one of these days be none of these days? Procrastination is dangerous if we're serious about recovery. Augustine was an exception. And he became a spiritual giant because he finally did bend his will to that of a Higher Power — not because he waited so long.

Today, I pray for the courage to take care of business. I will be aware that lost time is lost forever.

February 12

> *I am not bound to win, but I am bound*
> *to be true. I am not bound to succeed,*
> *but I am bound to live up to what light*
> *I have.*
> — *Abraham Lincoln*

There are as many definitions of success as there are people. Some want fame, some money — some fame *and* money. Some define success as professional attainment, some as personal popularity. These varying definitions identify all the gaps in our society — generation gaps, cultural gaps, educational gaps, credibility gaps. Each group has its own ideas about success.

Maybe the lack of a common understanding of success is the reason so many of us are alienated. Maybe we should all agree that real success is spiritual, not tangible. It is a matter of being ever more alive, not ever more effective about getting what we want. Greater life is a gift we can only give to ourselves and to one another. To be a giver is to be successful.

As I work my program today, I will focus my sights on inner rather than outer success. It doesn't matter if the world counts me a success; the important thing is that I do.

I was bitter about my parents until I realized how bitter they were about their parents.

— *Birdie V.*

Sometimes we adult children get wrapped up in our own family of origin and forget that everyone has a family of origin. Even our parents. Especially our parents, as a matter of fact.

It can be healing to reflect on our parents' early lives, what models were presented to them, and how they were expected to respond. Unlike us, they probably didn't have self-help books, groups or meetings, sponsors, or a program. They didn't have insights about lifelong progress toward a better self.

Someone has to break the vicious cycle. Resentment breeds resentment, and bitterness breeds bitterness. If we hated what we got from our parents, chances are that they, too, hated what they got from their parents. But no one broke the cycle, so it just kept rolling.

One day our own children may be working on their family of origin. That's something to think about, isn't it? How much will we hope for their understanding?

Today, I will think objectively about life cycles. I will live in the knowledge that my own children will one day judge me.

> *Genuine self love is the greatest protec-*
> *tion against dependent relationships.*
> — *Robert Coleman*

Adult children meetings can help male-dependent women who are struggling for emotional independence. As one woman shared, "I've taken any kind of treatment just to 'have a man.' To save my self-esteem, I've just ended a bad relationship. But it's still hard. Sometimes I feel so terrified I just want to run to him — but I haven't. Each day I stay put I count as a success."

Like many before her, this woman is learning the difference between love and dependency. She is thinking new thoughts and coming up with better options. In working her program, she is focusing on her own needs rather than someone else's. By acknowledging that she has always been accepted by her Higher Power, she is seeing her baby steps turn into a giant leap toward the independence of genuine self-worth.

I will learn to take care of myself, understanding that as I do so my vulnerability to dependent relationships lessens.

Why are we surprised when fig trees bear figs?
— *Margaret Titzel*

A frequent source of discomfort and pain with adult children is unrealistic expectations. One of the greatest of these is expecting sane, rational, trusting behavior from those who may well not have it to give.

Alcoholism is a form of insanity — perhaps not the commitable kind, but a disease that renders the victim incapable of behavior that most would call normal. Until the advent of recovery the alcoholic is subject to a bewildering assortment of delusions, denials, manipulations, and subterfuges. In short, nonrecovering alcoholics are incapable of functioning in healthy relationships.

When we expect anything more from a loved and beloved nonrecovering alcoholic, we are setting ourselves up for heartbreak. Fig trees bear figs, not peaches. What we are able to do emanates from what we are, not from what we wish we were.

Today, I will not frustrate myself with unrealistic expectations. What I cannot change, I will accept.

February 16

I spent my whole life thinking I was an exception. I never dreamed that everybody else was so much like me.
— *Teresa P.*

Discussion at our meetings can sometimes sound pretty strange. Everybody in the world seems clearly divided between "them" and "us." They are always different from us. Sometimes they are normal, and we are sick. And sometimes it's a reverse twist — they are somehow not as sensitive, worthy, or intelligent as we are. After all, they aren't working a program, which means they don't use our words or think the same as we do.

What are we doing when we talk ourselves into such dubious specialness? Does it make sense to draw a line between us and the rest of the human race? In fact, the idea of how different we are is a myth. Despite differences in specific details, we are more alike — in needing love and support, feeling lonely and scared, and yearning for the good fellowship of our peers — than we are different. All of us bleed if we're cut very deeply.

Today, I will search my heart for any trace of the snobbery of the wounded. I will remember that all people are wounded and thus deserving of compassion — just like me!

Fear is False Evidence Appearing Real.
                                    — Paula L.

There is no question that fear is a bully that is capable of totally paralyzing our lives. Fear pushes hard. Fear speaks in a loud, intimidating voice. Fear is powerful.

Yet nearly every fear we have is learned. Responding to one kind of evidence or another, we learned to fear the things we do. Fear is a self-fulfilling prophecy: A situation is presented as scary, we act scared, and the fear-caused consequences that result reinforce the fear we were taught to feel. The question is — how good was the evidence in the first place? Usually, it was false. Is it really true that people won't like us if we stand up for ourselves? Is it true that we won't have friends if we don't go along with the crowd? Is it true that all relationships will eventually fall apart?

There is no question why many of us learned to be so afraid. The evidence was there. But was it true?

Today, I can dispel my fears by remembering that good is at work in my life.

February 18

*Though patience be a tired mare, yet
she will plod.*
— *William Shakespeare*

Rare indeed is the person who doesn't need
much time to learn. And not only time — but
plenty of opportunity to make mistakes and more
mistakes until the lesson runs deep enough that
finally, we have it.

So many of us, though, have had the experience
of accepting crushing expectations, expectations
that made us stagger and fall. The result was a
devastated self-image. Perhaps someone in our
past expected us, unrealistically, to know immediately what we could only learn through trial and
error. So we failed.

Many of us carry that sense of failure with us on
through the years. No matter what we accomplish
or how quickly we accomplish it, it is never
enough to wipe out that early imprint, or so say
the ghosts from the past. Maybe it's time we asked
someone else.

*Today, I'll listen to words of encouragement from
friends and family who see the good in me.*

I got fed up with rewarding my illness.
It cost me too much.

— *Marvin H.*

To reward something indicates that we value it.
The payoff represents our hope that the same thing
will happen again. Rewards are encouragements
for repeat performances.

Unaware, we can very easily reward our own
illness. We do it by simply acting out our old,
destructive habits and patterns — by keeping them
with us, by practicing them. The more we act them
out, the less aware we become.

We reward illness when we feel afraid and then
let that feeling halt our action. When we allow our
shame to get the upper hand by getting into unrealistic expectations, we reward illness. When our
low self-esteem nudges us into relationships that
can only end in heartbreak, or when we allow
unacceptable behavior to go unchallenged, we are
rewarding illness.

We don't need to pay the high cost of feeding the
disease by repeating these self-defeating patterns.
We've paid enough for defeat; it's time to invest in
success.

Today, I will throw my energy into positive redi-
rection. Nothing I do today will cater to my illness.

> *God respects me when I work, but He
> loves me when I sing.*
> — *Rabindranath Tagore*

What image does the word God conjure up? For
many of us the word God simply throws up the
image of yesterday — unexamined, untested, un-
contested. Like so many other concepts, our old
idea of God needs to be considered again in the
light of recovery.

Many of yesterday's images would have God as
some stern, white-clad figure sitting above, casting
a critical eye on all we are and do. We may have
believed that God's only desire for us is that we
work hard and suffer bravely. Oftentimes, the God
of our childhood thinks work is all that counts.

Upon consideration, however, we may come to a
more enlightened, loving image of God. As we
learn more about what love is and looks like, we
may come to the understanding that what God
most wants for us is our happiness, contentment,
and peace. We may arrive at the lovely situation of
coming to understand that God is as happy with us
at play as He is with us at work. Or even more so.

*Today, I know that "God the taskmaker" was a
figment of my imagination. As I come to know
myself better, I am coming to know God better.*

Nothing great was ever achieved without enthusiasm.
— *Ralph Waldo Emerson*

Apathy is deadly. In the same way that caring is a sign of life, apathy or indifference suggests that emotional exhaustion is nearly complete. As long as we care, the flame still flickers and we have a chance. We may not be able to act very effectively on our problems, but as long as we care we are still able to take action.

Sometimes apathy seems to fall over us like a smothering blanket. Often it overtakes us when we are depressed, or when we've faced some situations so painful that we just don't have the energy to throw it off and lift our spirits. At these times it is helpful to picture someone or something we do care about. When we think about people and beliefs we hold dear, we can poke the dying fire to life by prodding the glowing embers of our concern. Like the sparks from those embers, our emotions too can crackle back to life. We can draw on the love around us to reenergize ourselves.

I can move out of my concern for myself and instead focus on those who are special to me. I will let them know I care.

> *As long as habit and routine dictate the*
> *pattern of living, new dimensions of*
> *the soul will not emerge.*
> — *Henry Van Dyke*

If nothing changes, nothing changes.

One reason people read books like this or throng to meetings is they want change — if not total change, then at least a modification of the portions of their lives that cause them distress. There are always reasons for our being stuck in the places we are. Those reasons are often our habits and patterns. If the painful consequences of whatever we find hurtful in our lives are frequent and recurring, we have a negative pattern.

As long as those habits and patterns remain unchallenged, of course there will be nothing new. Habits are like machines routinely, consistently, stamping out the same product year after year. They can do nothing else. They are made to create that specific product.

Change demands new behaviors, new thoughts, possibly new surroundings. Change demands the willingness to go to war with old habits. Frightening — yes. Exciting — even more so!

I am willing to risk the security of old ways for the
prospect of happy, new tomorrows.

What is strength without a double share of wisdom? Vast, unwieldy, burdensome, proudly secure, yet liable to fall.

— John Milton

What do we mean when we say someone is strong? That they have big muscles? Can endure anything without getting tired, let alone giving up? Do strong people never bend? Never break?

Some of us are afraid to show weakness of any kind. We take our supposed strength as the central fact of our lives. Over time, we may even come to think of ourselves as indestructible. We imagine that everything — people, places, and things — can be pounded into place if we come on with enough force. One man at a meeting shared that he had been confined to a hospital bed after a serious heart attack. Since he had been forbidden exertion of any kind, he said he made himself get out of bed, walk across the room, and pick up a scrap of paper from the floor. Just to prove that he could, he said.

Many of us are more like this man than we care to admit. May we, like him, become willing to accept our strength as our weakness, if that is the case.

Today, let me accept my very real and human limitations.

> *Sometimes things have to get worse before they get better.*
>
> — *Joe B.*

Oh, how we hate pain! Doesn't everyone? And it isn't true that pain is ennobling or in some other mysterious way "good for you." The only people who say that are those who have gotten by, so far, without much pain. But sometimes things have to get worse — more painful — before they get better.

We feel painful conflict when we start to recover. After all, we have lived in certain systems for many years. And these systems are self-perpetuating — they always seek stability. Sparks fly when we move in on our systems and start to change the rules. There is always confrontation when we act instead of react. And confrontation means challenge. In the midst of conflict and confusion, the pain of forging on can be almost unbearable. It would be so easy to throw in the towel and surrender. But sometimes there's just no way out but through. The rewards of discovering that path are great and will stay with us for a lifetime.

Today, I pray for courage to persist. If there has to be pain, let me accept it now, get on with it, and through with it.

Love bade me welcome:
  yet my soul drew back.
Built of dust and sin.
But Quick-ey'd love,
  observing me grow slack
From my first entrance in,
Drew nearer to me,
  sweetly questioning,
If I lack'd anything.

— *George Herbert*

A loving invitation is far more powerful than a sales pitch. When we welcome newcomers to the program, it is always appropriate to assure them that things can get better, that they can make them better. We must never give the impression that the task of recovering is easy if you just do it.

The demons behind some of our locked doors have been there for many years. These demons may conceal the death of another, a life spent on drugs, a corner in which to hide because the alternative was just too ugly to face. It is true that we have to face our demons in order to heal. But it is equally true that insensitivity can scare newcomers into backing off. A heartfelt "We're glad you're here" is a powerful message of hope.

Today, I will remember how it feels to look, for the first time, at the long path winding over the mountain.

February 26

*Patience, that blending of moral cour-
age with physical timidity . . .*
— *Thomas Hardy*

All beautiful things take time, their own time, to
grow. They run on their own clocks, not on ours.
Why do we have such unrealistic expectations
about progress? Why are we always so sure we
know how long it should take?

It is extremely common to hear an adult child at
a meeting say something like this: "I don't know
what's the matter with me. I must be mentally ill
or something. I keep taking one step forward and
two steps backward. I don't think I'm changing at
all. Why do I keep forgetting what works?" But
how fast should it be? Whose clocks are we timing
with? How long did it take us to develop our character flaws? How quickly do we imagine they can
be overcome? A big job takes a while to accomplish; it's as simple as that. We have no legitimate
reason for such impatience. There's no such thing
as being late. The time it takes is the time it has
needed. We'll get there.

*Today, I will be conscious of the growth that is
already mine and continue to patiently work my
program.*

I did it again! I feel terrible! I am terrible!

— *Jim E.*

Those thoughts were expressed in anguish at a meeting of adult children. The speaker was a young man who had been sober for three years. Abused as a child, Jim had been married while drinking and divorced while sober. After the pain of the breakup, Jim had resolved never to get involved again.

But Jim got lonely as time went on. He wanted love as we all want love. Then he met Julie. They fell in love. Jim became terrified. What he wanted most was what he feared most. The closer Julie came, the more Jim panicked.

Then one night, Jim reported, he picked a fight. "For no reason," he said. He cruelly pushed Julie away. He now wonders if Julie will ever talk to him again.

But there was a reason for the fight. Jim is at his adult child crossroads. Old patterns or new truths? Life and love or withdrawal and death? We all know where the old ways get us. We understand and we sympathize. But the time comes when each of us has to choose. Which way will it be?

Today, I will stand up against despair. I will have faith in myself in spite of my repeated failings.

> *Came to believe that a Power greater
> than ourselves could restore us to san-
> ity.*
> — *Step Two of* Alcoholics Anonymous

Having admitted powerlessness in the First Step,
we now begin to open our hearts and our minds to
a reality greater than ourselves. It takes time to
believe in the possibilities, time to exhaust all other
means of making our own light, and time to recognize our need for restoration. We have carried our
dysfunctional childhood patterns into adulthood
and have continued to live those patterns even
when they're no longer necessary. This is our insanity.

The sanity promised by the Second Step restores
the ability to think on our own and to act on today's decisions rather than those made decades ago
in a dysfunctional system. It is the sanity of inte-
gration — thoughts, actions, and feelings acting as
one — instead of the fragmented insanity of having our thoughts say one thing and our actions
doing just the opposite. We take this Step confident that our Higher Power can restore our ability
to live rationally.

*Perhaps for the first time in my life I am ready to
believe that help is available to me.*

Take away love and our earth is a tomb.

> — *Robert Browning*

Scientists have learned a lot about healthy brains by studying brains that have been injured. Certain injuries, they have found, produce certain dysfunctions. Each loss is a clue to how the functioning whole works. Each broken connection has a story to tell.

Particular behaviors also signal when our love connections break down. Here are some common dysfunctions: We pick at the faults in others that we most dislike in ourselves; we strike out when we feel most powerless; we try to make others feel guilty when our own feelings of guilt become intolerable. Damaged connections block love from going either way. All these behaviors are clues that we have had a vital loss, that our emotional well-being is under attack. A free flow of love is as necessary to the spirit as a free flow of blood is to the body.

I will keep my love healthy today by taking my own inventory and overlooking my loved ones' flaws.

March

Being alone is a markedly different experience than being lonely.
— *La Rochefoucaud*

There is great power and wisdom in growing to the point where silence becomes our friend. It is in silence that we best listen and a great portion of life's best secrets can only be learned in silence.

Those running from themselves and the hurtful lessons of the past fear silence more than any other reality. The fear is I may hear myself in that silence, and surely the sourness of that word would sicken me. Such people are always lonely — whether alone or surrounded by multitudes.

In reality, if we stand still and be quiet, the word we hear softly spoken in the inner court of our own castle, is full of beauty and loveliness. If we listen we will learn that we are not bad, that we are not disgusting, failure-ridden people, and we are not powerless. Quite the contrary, there is much that is right and noble about us.

Alone or lonely — it is a matter of courting silence or not.

Every day I take more pleasure in my own company.

March 2

I was born a girl. That was my original sin.

— Molly S.

It is unfair, one of the worst forms of injustice, to be penalized for something beyond our control. Especially when the people being punished are children. Many boys have struggled to meet their parents' expectations of masculinity, no matter how unrealistic or insensitive. Many girls are not taken seriously because of their sex. As children, we all wanted to be appreciated for what we were and to have our value recognized. Perhaps that acceptance never came.

We may have envied the dreamlike relationships some of our friends seemed to have with their parents. We saw the trusting look in our friends' eyes when their fathers were around, or we heard their mothers praising their school projects. We dreamed our own situation was like theirs. We pretended, lied, and built elaborate fantasies. But we knew it wasn't so.

Now irrational rejection is seen for what it was — a form of insanity. We no longer look for affirmation from those who are emotionally disabled. We look to each other — recovering men and women — for an accurate reflection of our worth.

I pray to forgive those who held me up to a distorted mirror.

> *All things work together for good to them that love God.*
>
> — *Romans 8:28*

Sometimes it's very hard to believe that God knows what He's doing. We are told to stop trying to control everything, so we do. We "Let Go," we "Turn It Over." We pry our grip off people, places, and things. As much as we want to hang on, we force ourselves to let God run the show. Then we wait and watch for the good things to start happening.

Most of the time events continue to unfold as unevenly as they always did. Accidents happen while setbacks, injustices, and evil get rewarded, and good goes begging. We feel that our letting go is mocked, that God isn't doing a better job than we did. Why isn't He performing?

But God can write straight with crooked lines. God's timetable may well not be the same as ours. What is asked is that we learn to believe without seeing and to trust when it seems we could do so much better.

Today, I pray for the faith to go the distance. Like a child leaping into a parent's arms, I know that I am too precious to drop.

March 4

> *Lives of great men all remind us*
> *We can make our lives sublime*
> *And, departing, leave behind us*
> *footprints on the sands of time.*
> — Henry Wadsworth Longfellow

Few of us ever think of ourselves as "great," and fewer still consider our lives "sublime." Yet there is no question that we will all depart life someday and leave some kind of footprints behind us. To our glory or regret, we all leave our marks.

Though we may not be aware of it, people do watch us. What we say and don't say, do and don't do, all have an effect on others. Our positive, hopeful attitude translates into encouraging applause for a struggling brother or sister, or our cutting remark may be the final douse of water on someone else's weak flame. Our actions and words do matter.

Let us look back at the footprints we have left so far. Do they lead toward recovery? It's not too late to strike out in a different direction.

For these twenty-four hours, I will set an encouraging example to those around me.

*No voice equals no choice. No choice
equals no power. From now on I want
to be heard.*

— *Dave C.*

Without a voice we don't have choice or power.
Children are the members of society who often
have no voice. Nearly all of us grew up to the tune
of "Children should be seen and not heard" or
some variation of that imperative. In our dysfunctional homes we learned that we, the children, had
no say in what happened. The result was devastating.

Unless we take conscious issue with them, the
crimes of the past repeat themselves in the present
and future. It is quite possible to grow old and die
marching along — blindly, silently, passively — to
the same sad tune piped to us in our youth.

But who says you and I should have no voice
today? Need we still give those people from our
past such power in our lives?

No matter how timid, unsure, or frightened we
feel, we must practice saying, "I am here. I count.
This is what I think." It is a wonderful, healthy
thing to stand up and speak out. We all deserve to
be heard.

*Today, I thank God for the miracle of finding my
own voice after being mute for so long.*

March 6

> *Wealth lost — something lost; Honor lost — much lost; Courage lost — all lost.*
>
> *— Old German Proverb*

Recovery is nothing to play around with. "Yesterday I felt like it; today I don't" might be a harmless enough attitude about whether or not we're going to learn to play the bongo drums, but it's masochistic to approach recovery that way.

There is no such thing as standing still. We either inch along forward or we slip backward. All that we have gained can be lost, and lost forever. Our lives are not soap operas. The issues we're dealing with are real, serious, and important. The stakes are high, and in some areas of our lives, unrecoverable.

On many a meeting room wall hangs a saying, "Never Compromise." The idea is not that we have to be perfect, but that every little slip is an invitation to a larger one. Recovery is so important that even the inches may become critical.

I will be on guard lest by ignoring the inches I find myself a mile off base.

*The truth shall set you free but first it
will make you miserable.*
                                        — Garfield

A young woman at a meeting said something
that is often heard from newly recovering people:
"Recovery created more problems than I had before." The more likely reality, of course, for her
and for all of us when we're just starting out, is not
that there are so many new problems, but that we
are now able to see old problems that we never
before saw.

Recovery creates insight — and with insight
comes heightened awareness of the need for decisions. Those decisions can hurt. They can call
from us the very strengths and skills we have the
least of and fear the most.

Before recovery we didn't have to make decisions because we didn't face our problems. After
recovery begins, sure, there will be some painful
decisions — but all the pain is growing pain.

*I can look for ways to deal with my problems,
rather than ways to avoid them.*

March 8

I may not be there yet, but I'm closer than I was yesterday.
— *Susie McD.*

Many adult children, for very understandable reasons, feel unworthy, guilty, and ashamed much of the time. We may feel a kind of gnawing at our self-esteem that makes it hard for us to see our own progress. We may be afraid to feel good.

It takes courage to look back down the road to see how far we have come toward daylight. But the rewards are great. When we give ourselves credit for all the progress, desire, and willingness to investigate the dark corners of our souls, we have good cause to celebrate who we are!

Facing up to and facing down the demons of guilt and low self-esteem require great courage. And when we can look not only backward but forward — our task is more courageous still.

It's not where we came from, or even where we are, that tells the story. It's where we are headed that gives rise to hope and the joyous shout, "I'm getting there! I'm doing just fine!"

Today, I will be grateful for the freedom I am capable of claiming and, in fact, am claiming every day I work my program.

Sow a thought, and you reap an act;
Sow an act, and you reap a habit;
Sow a habit, and you reap a
   character;
Sow a character, and you reap a
   destiny.

— Samuel Smiles

God provides food for every bird but He doesn't place it in the nest. God provides for us too. We are surrounded by marvelous sources of wisdom — the sharing of other adult children, spiritual readings, the practical Steps of the program — everything we need to heal and grow! But just as the birds must find and gather the food that has been provided, so also must we act if the gift is to be brought home.

We must use what we have learned. Without action, all the wise insights in the world won't put us in a better place. If insight tells us that feelings of shame don't need to be acted out — we must stop. If we've discovered a tendency to get involved in lose-lose relationships — we must resist.

It's not what we know that will make a difference. It's what we do with what we know.

I am practicing the strong habits of the program in order to use what has been provided.

March 10

Compassion is daring to acknowledge our own destiny so that we might move forward together.
— *Henri Nouwen*

Thank God for our friends in the program! Especially those who started out before we did, who were waiting for us when we came in. How else could we know that fear was the problem? Who else could have shown us that fear could be faced? Because they had faced their own fear, they could see beyond our mask of loud talk, constant boasting, and flippant put-downs. They could see through all that because they'd already seen the lost child in their own eyes.

Because they admit and accept their own failures, they are neither too permissive nor too hard on the failures of others. They know the truth — that failure is a part of life. Because they themselves have tasted tragedy, they are blessedly free of the judgments, the all-knowing verdicts, passed down by so many others. May we always be grateful for these people who knew us and loved us before they even met us!

Today, I pray that every good thing will come to the generous people who invited me to come along.

You're only as sick as your secrets.
> — *Kay B.*

To think is to discover what's in the head. To share is to discover what's in the heart. In truth, we often don't know exactly what we think and feel until we share it with another. It is through the mysterious, subtle, powerful act of sharing that we can muster the courage to shed our fears. It is by asking for and gaining the support of others that we can dare to stand up in the sunshine with the rest of God's creatures.

Our friends in the program can't know what we don't tell them. They aren't mind readers. And they aren't deserving of our resentment and anger, which they often get, for not responding to a problem we didn't share with them. "Why don't they see?" we may whine to ourselves. "I have helped many of these people in their times of need. Now they're letting me bleed to death. Do I have to die before someone notices?"

No. Probably all we have to do is tell them. If we let them know what's happening, we'll be amazed to find they were there for us all the time.

Today, I will challenge all of my reasons for not sharing. I will give sharing — and myself — a chance.

March 12

> *Loneliness expresses the pain of being alone and solitude expresses the glory of being alone.*
> — *Paul Tillich*

It may be said the road that runs between loneliness and solitude is the highway of recovery. Before recovery most of us fear and flee loneliness. We may be terrified of being alone because we don't think of ourselves as good company. Once the walk down the road of recovery has begun, however, we discover in that same aloneness a most marvelous person — ourselves.

Our task is to resist the old, infernal messages that would make us shy away from ourselves. Our task is to rise above that horrid noise and acknowledge that we have marvelous thoughts if we would only give ourselves credit for them. We need to accept that many people love us, and their lives would be less if we were not part of them. We love and are loved. That makes us very special.

It is not the stillness that matters, for that is the same in both loneliness and solitude. The difference is in the attitude we have toward ourselves.

As my recovery grows, so does my ability to be comfortable in my own company.

*Once I accept things as they are I can
create things as they might be.*
— Mike O.

Nothing so ties us to the past as regret. Think about it. It is almost impossible to venture forth while facing backward.

But today's reality is what we must accept and work with. What was is gone. All we can do in the here and now is to accept it as it is without rage or blame, without regret or resentment. All the voting has already been done that made today be what today is.

Ah, but the future! Tomorrow! That's quite a different matter. Today we vote for what tomorrow will be. Today's seeds are tomorrow's harvest, today's struggle is tomorrow's victory.

When we accept today as it is without regret, we shuck off the terrible burden of self-pity with all its "shoulds," "if onlys," and "what ifs." A thousand "ifs" don't equal a single "is." When we build on accepted reality, we build on solid rock.

Now I choose. From this day forward, the choice is mine!

March 14

The great good God looked down and smiled and counted each His loving child, for monk and Brahmin, Turk and Jew, loved Him through the gods they knew.

— *Alfred, Lord Tennyson*

Sharing with another human being is called communication. Sharing with God is called prayer. There are different manners of praying, different times of praying, and different names used for the Higher Power. We don't all need to pray the same way — but we all need prayer.

Prayer works. An endless river of examples flows through our meetings and reflects that truth: Prayer works. At a tense time, a fearful time, a hard or a confused time, a time of celebration or thanksgiving — someone prayed. God was sought, the mental and spiritual doors were opened with a simple, "Help me, be with me," and that presence was there.

As feeble and hesitant as our efforts at conscious contact may be, God will bring the party to us if we only invite Him.

I will reach out to God no matter how doubtful or undeserving I feel.

*Thank God every morning when you
get up that you have something to do
which must be done, whether you like
it or not.*
— *Charles Kingsley*

Marshall McLuhan warned that this age of electronic marvels could turn out to be less than marvelous for human development. He predicted that one effect would be the spawning of vast numbers of voyeurs — people who would rather watch than participate, seek vicarious rather than real experiences, and seemingly not know the difference.

We all know (or may be) people who would rather watch television than participate in the living drama of today's world. Being a spectator is safe. The secondhand defeats and triumphs, the loves and losses that flicker across the screen don't require that we take a stand or make an effort. As long as we don't participate, we don't have to make decisions or take risks.

But real life is lived in the trenches, and real action is never secondhand. As the years go by and we look back on our lives, will we want to remember that we played the game? Or that we played it safe?

Today, I pray for the courage to get involved in my own drama.

March 16

Father, how could you? Why didn't you? If only you would have . . .
— Glen D.

For adult children, the word *father* often represents a reality that is both powerful and confusing. For some of us it is the father we never had. For others it is the father we wish we never had. Perhaps it is the sun that never shone warm enough to ward off the chill, the voice from on high that never spoke through all the years that we waited, listening.

We were taught to pray "Our Father," and we did. But for many of us, our prayers were pretend words out of a fairy tale. When we said them, we felt only a void and a sense of confusion. Many of the fathers in our homes were unable to provide us with the comfort, security, and warmth we needed to grow.

But we do have a Father who knows our needs, recognizes our hopes, and understands our losses. He is unchanging, unfailing, incapable of human failure. Our Father calls each of us by name. We are not abandoned.

Today, I will be open to a different, greater reality than I perceived in the past. I will learn to take comfort in the Fatherhood of God.

> *God offers to every mind its choice between truth and repose. Take which you please — you can never have both.*
> — *Ralph Waldo Emerson*

Denial is sneaky and hard to detect. Like a chameleon, a denied reality tends to change color until it blends right in and seems to fit. Since we don't have to deal with what we don't see, we camouflage some truths that we're afraid will hurt or challenge us.

Some of us deny that anyone else ever lived in a family as dysfunctional as ours, or, that our families were dysfunctional at all. Others insist only their siblings were affected, or only themselves. We may tell ourselves we're deliberating when we're really procrastinating. The varieties of self-deception are almost limitless.

Our talent for denial is an important reason for making friends in the program. We need people we can trust enough to tell us the truth — loving people who will say what needs to be said, even if it's uncomfortable at first to hear.

I recognize my need for honest feedback. I'm less afraid of openness than I used to be.

March 18

Judge a man by his questions rather than by his answers.

— *Voltaire*

To learn more about anything is to become increasingly able to make meaningful observations: "Aha! That's why the teacher said to do it this way!" or "Now I get it! It's this command, not that one, that runs the program!" In large part, to know the difference is to know the right questions.

We can't change the fact of a divorce, for example, but we can deal more creatively with loneliness. If we're short, we can't make ourselves taller, but we can learn to deal with insensitive jokes. If someone has died, we can't make that person live again, but we can do something about the despair we may feel. What's the correct question? Will God reverse what has happened? Or is the question really this: Will God give us the spiritual power to deal with what is?

If we have been asking that God spare us pain, perhaps we should try a different question: Will God lead us through our pain to a greater understanding of life?

I will learn to trust more in my Higher Power and the direction He gives my life.

*I finally figured out that my dad's opin-
ion was no better than his information.
And his information was wrong.*
— Dana J.

Until we embrace recovery, our opinion of ourselves is often based on faulty information. Usually, this is information we got long ago from people who didn't know the truth about what life
could be, about their own worth and value, or
about the beauty of other people. When we received that faulty information, we used it to form
an opinion not only of ourselves, but of other people and the world around us. Too often those opinions hardened into "facts," and those "facts" en-
tombed us in the past.

We adult children are called to break out of that
hardened emotional cement. We are called to understand the truth — that those who gave us that
faulty information did not always know what the
truth was. They just passed on what was passed to
them.

We come to see a new truth: The world around
us is largely made up of our own attitudes.

*Today, I ask myself: Are my opinions really mine
or were they given to me by someone else? On
what truths are these opinions based?*

> *If winter comes, can spring be far be-*
> *hind?*
> — *Percy B. Shelley*

In the seasonal predictability of nature, we can always be certain that spring follows winter. But this is not so in human matters.

Those of us with a healthy attitude and loving support may endure profound distress, go on to heal, and perhaps even gain precious wisdom as a result of this experience. Like seasonal changes, this is a passing from death to life.

For some of us, however, there is no passage to life, only from one stage of dying to another. Too few lessons have been learned, too little wisdom has been gained for the wound to heal.

There is nothing natural or guaranteed about a springtime of the spirit. We must choose it. That we can is the glorious part. To work the program is to choose the season in which we live.

I will claim the power that is mine to choose the attitude by which I live.

*When spring comes the grass grows by
itself.*

— *The Tao*

People who don't know how to relax have a very
rough row to hoe in this world. Adult children,
perhaps, need to learn to relax more than anyone
else.

Many of us live by one overriding code: Do
more, do it better, do it faster. Since no one probably taught us that in so many words, we practiced
it until it became a rule of perfection and took up
residence in the control room of our being. We fail
at our projects unless we work harder than everyone ever has, have greater success, and accomplish
it sooner. And the most excellent outcome, of
course, is not good enough. The rule of perfectionism makes it impossible for us to enjoy success.

When we apply the hurry-up rule to our own
recovery, we brand ourselves fools, failures, and
frauds if we don't get freedom from the old bondage *now*.

But immediate recovery is impossible. The only
thing we need to do immediately is to relax.

*I am learning to say no to the inner voice that
demands superhuman efforts.*

March 22

*We may be the only Easter lily some
people ever see.*
— *Rev. R. Oelerich*

Regardless of how strange it may sound, we are
powerful people! We make a difference in others'
lives, for good or ill. We enhance people's lives
when we encourage, support, and congratulate. It
is easy to downplay the importance of our lifting
up our fellow pilgrims even though it is no small
thing when we are the beneficiaries of such life-
giving gifts.

The newspaper ran a story of a teenaged girl
who had been a prostitute. The account was
mostly an interview in which she repeatedly told
of how she had been put down at home, was made
to feel she didn't count, was denied affection, and
came to believe that what she did mattered little
because no one cared.

The story of her life-style change came as a
result of a hard-won battle by a social worker who
unfailingly mirrored back to the girl that she did
count, and that she was a person filled with love
and beauty. Perhaps neither the parents nor the
social worker would think of themselves as powerful, but in this case they made all the difference.

*Today, I will be aware that I make a difference. I
will make the world a little better for my being in
it.*

*In thy face I see the map of honor,
truth, and loyalty.*
> — *William Shakespeare*

People choose their mates for many reasons — the irresistable twinkle in a young man's eye, the graceful curve of a woman's ankle, escape from home, to have a home, financial support, convenience — you name it. But to stay alive, a relationship has to have something else, something more basic going for it. It has to have trust.

Bedrock trust means that we know the other person is in our corner, reliably there for us no matter what. It means that in significant ways, they are "present" to us. If they are not, no matter how much we think we need them or how desperately we want the relationship to work, no trust equals no satisfaction.

Until the other proves trustworthy (beyond promises and good intentions) something in us holds back. Some aspects of the relationship may well be terrific, but the lasting test is always, "Can I trust them?"

Today, I am proud of the ways in which others trust me.

March 24

Every battered child grew up in poverty.

— *Mack M.*

Battering takes many forms. It often is physical, certainly, but it can also be emotional or spiritual. All battering leaves scars in the spirit of a child.

Many of us don't remember being battered. Having never looked at the poverty of our early emotional environment, we sometimes assume our current distress is of our own making. If the blows we endured weren't physical, we tend to think of them as something else. Or we don't think of them at all.

But nearly every child who thinks he doesn't count is a child needing love. And a child who is convinced she can't do anything right is a child living in poverty. Knowing we are adequate and worthy is fundamental to sane living. It is our birthright to know ourselves as glorious, innocent creations. Deprivation of that birthright is poverty in its most serious form.

Being born into a poor emotional environment need not sentence us to a lifetime of spiritual poverty. The past was not our choice — the present is.

I am responsible for the world I live in today. I will not define my life by yesterday's wounds.

The price of wisdom is above rubies.
— Job 28:18

Our program is founded on wisdom, and the wisdom of the program is the light of our lives. It shines into the dark corners of the spirit where the myths lurk that would degrade rather than create, entrap rather than set free. Wisdom lets us see what and whose game is being played. Is it my game or yours? Not to know the difference is to dangle like a puppet from a set of strings hooked to head and limbs.

It may be a game of guilt, of taking responsibility for someone else's life, of accepting peace at any price — or any number of enslaving games. Without the wisdom of the program, how could we know? Without wisdom, how could we learn to give ourselves credit for how far we have come rather than berate ourselves for how slow we are moving? What a relief and a comfort to be able to rely on our wise Steps and Traditions for failsafe guidance.

Today, I am grateful for the program's teachings.

March 26

Made a decision to turn our will and our lives over to the care of God as we understood Him.

— Step Three of
Alcoholics Anonymous

Turn it over is a phrase we hear a lot in a Twelve Step setting. It does not mean abandon or dump. Nor does it mean that forever onward we are somehow not responsible for the lives we turn over.

The God that we understand today is not some-one else's image of God that was forced on us, perhaps years ago. Today, whatever our under-standing, God is more than just a sad reflection of imperfect, human authority. The program teaches, and the Third Step states, that the God of our understanding is a caring God. While we've not had the best experience of being well-cared for by those more powerful than ourselves, the Third Step assures us that we can have that experience now.

To turn our lives and wills over to such a God is an act of considered, intelligent judgment and of courageous, confident trust. It is an acknowledg-ment of the reality that we really can't run the show ourselves.

Today, I am able to make an important commit-ment in spite of any fearful feelings.

People have the right not to recover.
— Lauren B.

Our best intentions and most diligent efforts may well not achieve the very object of our desire, especially if what we most desire is the recovery of our loved ones. No matter how much we want them to be healthy and whole, no matter how much information we give them or how much help we offer — they have the right not to recover.

No one can force anyone else to change. We can't get inside other people's heads and make their choices for them. Decisions that make a difference emanate from free will. They come from the inside, not the outside; they are personal, not social.

The example of our lives is the most powerful tool we have in such situations. The only force that may have an influence is the moral force of a life lived with serenity and truth. All we can do is let the light of the program shine through us, and pray that the curtains blocking the light will somehow, some day, be drawn back so the light can enter.

I am comforted by knowing that my afflicted loved ones are beloved children of God, and He will care for them.

March 28

Only with a true friend's input can we hope to see our world clearly, for our own perception always seems the truth.
— *Dr. Richard Fritz*

We need our friends. Not just for good times but for basic health. In isolation, everything becomes magnified. Without others to help us form our boundaries and perceptions, whatever we can imagine becomes monstrous and whatever is monstrous becomes reality.

If our old rules tell us to hold back and to decline closeness, we put ourselves at risk when we obey. Lacking the shared experience of others, we are vulnerable, not only to loneliness, but to gross misinterpretation of reality. Minor setbacks may be seen as catastrophic, and people who don't go out of their way to be friendly may be plotting against us.

By connecting with friends, however, we're able to see that our monsters are only about knee-high, that most of our fears are made of smoke, and that no gray day can hold out against the sunshine of common sense and a functioning program.

I am thankful for the stabilizing influence of friends.

The lust for power, for dominating others, inflames the heart more than any other passion.

— *Tacitus*

We know that Mary loves John because she worries about him so much. She anticipates his every wish, spares him every inconvenience, and binds his wounds before he even knows he's hurt. Managing John's life, in fact, is Mary's full-time job. She works hard at it and she hasn't got time for much else.

Most of the time Mary feels satisfied with the choices she has made in life. She's proud of the efficiency and order that reigns in their home. Mary doesn't like loose ends or unresolved situations, and in her world, they don't exist. John seems happier now than he did when Mary first took charge. Until Mary convinced him to sit back and take it easy, he seemed strangely resentful and angry about every little aspect of her organizational plan. But he got over it. Now he dozes a lot in front of the TV while Mary works on her lists.

Peace at any price doesn't give genuine peace. Genuine peace comes from making choices that create more life, not less.

Today, I will examine my decisions to be sure I haven't traded compliance for integrity.

March 30

*When they didn't love me, I thought
there was something wrong with me.*
— *Donna B.*

Children see with the eyes of children and think with children's minds. They don't have much experience, after all.

When we felt unloved, we didn't have the sophistication to wonder whether our parents loved themselves. We didn't have any way of knowing that loving has much more to do with the capacity of the giver than it does with the deservedness of the receiver. Children don't reason that way. "If you don't hold me," we assumed, "it must be that I am not holdable. Others kids are loved. The fault must be with me."

We are not children now. As we mature, we can gain the insight to understand, to take responsibility for sorting out what was from what is. We can ask for support when we need it.

Now we know there wasn't anything wrong with us. Not back then, and not now. Knowing this, we are able to forgive and let go — to move on. We deserve to be loved, just as we always did. We don't have to think with the mind of a child anymore.

I will develop my ability to love and be loved by associating with people who are capable of love.

*Through our own recovered innocence
we discern the innocence of our neighbors.*

— *Henry David Thoreau*

From time to time we get tired of hearing the
word community. Perhaps the word itself has been
overused to the point of meaninglessness. Or perhaps deep inside we fear that the community will
rob us of our individuality. But that just isn't so.
Both a community and a crowd are made up of
individuals. The difference is in the way the individuals react to one another.

A mob is mindless — it doesn't matter who its
members are. A community, on the other hand, is
authentic because it's made up of separate, distinct
people. Without the diverse relationships within
the group, a would-be community could never get
off the ground.

Within the growing community of adult children, all members are unique, valued, and accepted "as is." We are one because we are many.

*I am comforted by seeing the good within us all,
because that means I am finding more worthwhile
qualities within myself.*

April

God grant me the serenity
to accept the things I cannot change,
courage to change the things I can,
and wisdom to know the difference.
— *Reinhold Niebuhr*

Some things I cannot change: my age, who my relatives are, my eye color, my height, my childhood experiences, my inborn talents, my nature, someone else's abuse of alcohol or drugs, whether the sun will shine, my job history, what I will inherit, how my parents feel, yesterday's lost opportunities, how long I will live, who forgives me, how my parents treated me, how much I am loved, the past.

Some things I can change: the youthfulness of my spirit, who my friends are, my hair color, my weight, my adult experiences, my achievements, my character, my reaction to someone else's use of alcohol or drugs, whether my eyes will shine, my job possibilities, what I will bequeath, how I feel, my ability to act on today's opportunities, how well I will live, whom I forgive, how I treat my own children, how much I love, the future.

I thank God for my growing ability to choose.

April 2

Life is eternal; and love is immortal;
and death is only a horizon; and a hori-
zon is nothing save the limit of our
sight.
— *Rossiter Worthington Raymond*

Whether we are religious or not, the essence of the Easter story is relevant to all of us. It is the triumphant message that light is more powerful than dark, that love is stronger than fear, and that life can win over death.

In all of us there are the seeds of darkness, despair, and death. Some adult children have lived their whole lives in the fear of being overwhelmed one day. For us, Easter is the symbol of ultimate victory made possible by a Power greater than ourselves. It is the celebration of our connection with that Higher Power.

No matter what our religious beliefs, the Easter story is not only about what happened to someone else; it's about what's happening to us — or can happen. It's about the experience of being lifted up and made new, when we ourselves didn't have the power to do it.

I believe that new life is possible through the power of a loving God.

The good life is a process, not a state of being. It is a direction, not a destination.

— *Carl Rogers*

Not only the good life, but all life, is a process. If we get a clear enough picture, we can see that nothing happens all at once, nothing totally "isn't" and then totally "is." That part of us that generates pain and fear came into being over time. We didn't get fearful all at once, but bit by bit, experience by experience. Part of us learned to expect the worst, to cringe in hiding, to settle for crumbs.

Developing a healthy, comfortable way of life is likewise a process. The part of us that expects improvement, that dares to stand tall and demand our rights, also builds up bit by bit over time. That's why it's so important to celebrate every success, no matter how small. The direction is right this time. We have every reason to expect health and happiness. As long as we're moving ahead, we're getting there.

I accept the fact that life is a journey. I've given up the delusion that an "arrival" is necessary for happiness.

April 4

*If a child lives with approval, he learns
to live with himself.*
— *Dorothy Law Nolte*

It has been said and proven over and over that a person's self-image is largely formed by the image reflected back from other people. Those around us are mirrors. The more important they are to us, the more power they have to reflect our identity back to us. Thus the world is largely in the process of being created daily before our own eyes.

We are the most important people in the world to our children. Their identity, as we reflect it back to them, is the first and the most important information they receive.

Despite the powerlessness we adult children may feel, let us also be aware of the enormous power we have in creating the self-image of our children. If we doubt this, all we need to do is recall the influence our parents had upon us in forming our self-image. We have the same power over our children. As we were influenced then, so we influence now. A miracle is happening before our eyes if we but see it.

I will lose no opportunity to show my children how beautiful they are.

Of course I prayed — and did
* God care?*
He cared as much as on the air
A bird had stamped her foot
And cried "Give me!"
                    — Emily Dickinson

Children are good examples of what emotional maturity isn't. Their whole well-being often hinges on the desire of the moment, whether it be an overpriced toy, making the football team, or buying a certain kind of prom dress. "Now" is the only time there is and the desired object or event is the only thing worth thinking about. To a child, disappointment doesn't look or feel like a passing setback; it seems like permanent devastation.

Are we so different? Don't we sometimes get just as obsessed with certain, coveted outcomes? Don't we kick and scream and stamp our feet, internally at least, when certain wishes are frustrated?

People who aren't very old have every right to be immature. On the other hand, we often can enjoy the benefits of such maturity only after we have paid the price of getting there.

I am growing more comfortable with doing the best I can and taking life as it comes.

April 6

I'm a lot less hard on myself these days.
I've realized that my demons are really
angels that have gone astray.
— Manny J.

"Oh no! Not something else to work on!"

How often we feel discouraged when we become aware of yet another self-defeating pattern in our lives. "Who needs this much awareness?" we may wonder.

Yet, many of these frustrating patterns are rooted in a healthy, love-centered search for what is beautiful. We are all born reaching for love. The family system we were born into was the "school" where we learned what we know about filling our needs. Some of these lessons led us down the wrong path. In our search for truth, we may have learned to lie. In our search for good feelings, we may have learned not to feel at all. Wanting the best, we sometimes learned the worst. But the worst was learned in search of the best. We are better, much better, than the sum of our flaws.

I will learn to accept my frustrations for what they are: the result of my attempts to meet real and legitimate needs.

Never find your delight in another's misfortune.
> — *Pubililius Syrus*

The German word *schadenfreude* means "delight in the troubles of another." How many of us are guilty, in greater or lesser degree, of this unattractive habit of thinking? Sometimes, perhaps, it is sheer boredom that makes us perk up at news of someone else's calamity. A fire, for instance, or a bad car accident often draws a crowd of onlookers who are more excited than they are empathetic.

But some of us actually find it more satisfying to observe another's misfortunes than her triumphs. We're quick to condemn and slow to commiserate. We don't mind a bit when people "get what's coming to them." We like to see people "knocked off their high horse." Which assumes that we know two things we don't know: 1) all the facts and 2) what anybody deserves. Schadenfreude is a canker in the heart. If we find it there, we must root it out at once.

I will wish others well that I may reap what I sow.

April 8

Often the test of courage is not to die,
but to live.

— *Orestes*

Some life situations can be so bitter, so devastating, we simply wish we had the courage to die rather than face them anymore. How much courage would it take, we may wonder, to just end it all? But courage is not the right word. In truth, it takes more courage to live than it does to die. To take up the broken pieces of our lives, to stand fast against our destructive patterns of thought and behavior without giving in — this is courage of the highest order.

In our worst depressions it takes courage to call a friend, go to a meeting, read inspirational literature. And we can find that courage. We can learn, with the help of God as we understand God and of those who love us, to count our blessings, to consider what is right with us and the world, to discover all the love that surrounds us.

The debilitating boundaries we have learned cannot confine us if we don't back off. Sheer courage, and courage alone, is what it takes to move those boundaries into healthier territory.

Today, I will say yes to life, yes to love, yes to my own power to make positive decisions.

I worry that I'm not normal. Then I worry that I don't even know what "normal" is.

— Hugh M.

Many of us struggle with fears of not being normal, of not being like other people. But what does the word really mean? For most of us, normal means whatever we have been feeling and doing long enough to become comfortable with.

Many of us adult children have practiced feeling nothing — that has become normal. Some of us have practiced feeling guilty for so long that we don't know what it means to feel confident. Others of us are so good at working, that playing seems unworthy of responsible adults — it's not normal.

Since feelings wrap themselves around behavior, we come to feel that many abnormal behaviors are perfectly normal. So we end up feeling normal only when we're doing something that is self-defeating. Conversely, to act on our own behalf, to become our own best friend, may feel anything but normal. For us, "What's healthy?" is a better question than "What's normal?"

Today, I will not worry about meeting somebody else's standards. I will make healthy choices, confident that they will become healthy patterns, and "normal" for me.

April 10

None preaches better than the ant. And
she says nothing.
— *Benjamin Franklin*

Many of us just love to preach. Even though we hated being preached at and may well have made solemn vows never to preach when we got older, we became preachy people in spite of ourselves. Now that we are older, we may find a pulpit everywhere we go.

But the best preaching has always been by example. The most powerful messages spring from who we are, not what we say. The most effective tool we have to make others "see the light" is to see the light more clearly ourselves.

Far better than to complain about never being thought about is to show others how wonderful such consideration is by giving them the gift of kindness. Better than preaching about a negative attitude is to light up our world with our own positive frame of mind. Better than to shout against intolerance is to display a live-and-let-live attitude ourselves.

Today, I will make sure my loudest sermons are the quality of my own life.

Great men are they who see that spiritual is stronger than any material force, that thoughts rule the world.
— *Ralph Waldo Emerson*

So much in our world is not pretty. So many awful things happen to innocent people. So many bad people seem to be in controlling situations. But are these people really bad, or are they blind? Are they filled with evil, or are they empty of spirituality, blind to spiritual truth?

As we grow older and more sophisticated, we often grow hard. We can become "realistic" in looking at misery and injustice. Something in us says, "So be it" — as if there were no other way it could be. We stop looking and so choose blindness.

But "So be it" can mean something else. It can mean we have recognized that the state of our world is a reflection of the state of human spirituality. It can mean we have decided to throw our weight against submission to the kind of thinking that accepts the unacceptable. "So be it" can be our declaration of war against spiritual blindness.

In an effort to see clearly I will speak out against injustice, and I will applaud beauty.

> *Bread of deceit is sweet to man: but afterwards his mouth shall be filled with gravel.*
> — *Proverbs 20:17*

Going "the third way" means allowing oneself to act dishonestly in a relationship. It means while in a committed, primary relationship, we enter a new relationship without breaking the old one. It also can mean allowing ourselves to be that other party. The third way means we are willing to compromise.

How does this happen? If we're not habitually honest in our communications, we can easily hint to another that we're interested and willing to be involved on a level where we're not free to be involved. The other's flattering response may make us feel wanted and important. So we go on step-by-step until we are deeply involved in a damaging situation.

The price of the third way trip is always high. It costs us self-esteem, increased shame and guilt, and a daily toll of anxiety. And always, always, the certitude that at some point, the fiddler must be paid.

My relationships can be honest. I owe that to myself and those I care about.

Let the dead Past bury its dead!
— Henry Wadsworth Longfellow

Like a rearview mirror, feelings face backwards. They show what's behind us — not where we are now, and not where we're going. The way we feel now has been conditioned by lessons we learned in the past. Our habitual feelings are reflections of where we've been and who we've been with.

It may be that we learned to feel guilty when we ask for what we need. If we learned the lesson well, we do indeed feel guilt everytime we claim a right. Perhaps we learned that we're supposed to feel suspicious and nervous if too many good things happen — and so we do.

As we recover, we can't use these old feelings as guides. We need to forge new ways of thinking, behaving, and feeling. We need to choose sane, healthy behavior no matter how we feel. And we need to send our feelings back to school by persisting in that behavior until the new lessons are learned as well as the old ones.

I now know that today's actions are the seeds of tomorrow's feelings. Today, I wait in joyful hope.

April 14

> They *may not deserve forgiveness, but*
> I *do.*
>
> — *Anne P.*

Forgiveness is an act, not a feeling. Though it may generate feelings, forgiveness is an exercise of the will. When we forgive, we refuse to be further damaged by the wrongdoing of others.

A refusal to forgive is called a resentment. And the victim of resentment is always the one who carries it. The people we refuse to forgive may neither know nor care about our resentment.

To hang onto a resentment is to harbor a thief in the heart. By the minute and the hour, resentment steals the joy we could treasure now and remember forever. It pilfers our energy to celebrate life — to face others as messengers of grace rather than ambassadors of doom. We victimize ourselves when we withhold forgiveness.

Today, I will remember that forgiveness is a giver and resentment is a taker. Because I deserve it, I will forgive old hurts. I will see forgiveness as a gift to myself.

Whatever you can do, or think you can, begin it. Boldness has genius, power and magic in it.

— *Goethe*

We do not have to be perfectly certain before acting. We do not have to feel perfectly confident about the outcome of our behavior. In fact, more times than not when we see people acting with what seems to be supreme confidence, it may indeed be an act. Which doesn't matter. What matters is that inertia was overcome.

In our recovery there will surely be many times when we encounter situations where our thoughts and actions fill us with anything but confidence. Regardless of our uncertainty we need to act boldly, and we need to trust our judgment. Boldness does have genius in it, and magic — the magic of proving to ourselves that we can do what is needed when the time is right. When that is possible, the whole world is within our grasp.

If I can act boldly on one small matter, I can act boldly on two. If I can act boldly on small matters, I can act boldly on large matters. If I keep going, I can't be stopped.

*Love cures people. Both the ones who
give it, and the ones who receive it.*
— *Karl Menninger*

What do we want out of recovery? Ten people
asked usually give ten different answers. Freedom,
maturity, relief from pain, experiencing self, and
healing the wounded child are just a few of the
classic answers. And each one is certainly a valid,
compelling reason to keep on going when the work
of recovery seems to involve more perspiration
than inspiration.

Yet we must not forget that there is one goal of
recovery that takes in and transcends all others.
This is that we *become better able to love and be
loved.* We can accomplish many things in life, but
the history of human experience tells us that, without
love, all other rewards are hollow.

The more we focus our recovery efforts on becoming
more capable of sharing in healthy relationships,
the more efficient our recovery efforts
will be. Especially for adult children, the fullest
experience of love is and will always be the ultimate
quest.

*I am healing and becoming whole. I have more to
bring to a relationship than I used to.*

> *I didn't know I'd have to tear down be-*
> *fore I could build up.*
> > — *Eleanor F.*

Why should recovery, which we want, be such a struggle? Usually, reaching out for what we want takes far less effort. But recovering is not just a matter of *doing* something, but of undoing what we've spent years building up.

We are experts at being afraid to stand up for ourselves, at feeling guilty for giving ourselves a break, and at panicking when things work out *too* well. For many of us, those feelings are as much a part of us as our fingerprints.

Now we are training ourselves to go against some strong feelings. We are doing what it takes to get what we want despite our feelings. The problem is that our feelings are *us*. Just as the desire and struggle for recovery are *us*. It's civil war!

No wonder recovery is a struggle. And the issue can't be whether or not it will hurt; it will. The issue is — which path will take us where we want to go, one step at a time?

Today, I pray for the courage to live with inner conflict. I will not frustrate myself by expecting recovery to be easy.

April 18

Worry never robs tomorrow of its sorrow; it only saps today of its strength.
— *A. J. Cronin*

Many adult children are expert worriers. No topic is so small that we can't blow it up into something big. The merest hint of an ill wind can trip the hair-trigger mechanism that gets us going. It takes years to develop such a reflex. Originally, we may have legitimately worried that what we loved would be taken from us or never be given to us in the first place.

But worry can become a way of life — we may not know how to live any other way. In the grips of this delusion, we might assume that if we don't worry about something, it will happen for sure. As if worry had the power to ward off tragedy! We might as well wear garlic around our necks to repel evil spirits.

As opposed to cautious realism, chronic worry is indiscriminate and irrational. We don't worry about disasters because they're so likely to happen — we worry because that's what we know how to do. Worry doesn't prevent the loss of anything except our own peace of mind.

I recognize that habitual worry is a learned response from long ago. Today I choose serenity.

There is nothing either good or bad,
but thinking makes it so.
— William Shakespeare

Is the glass half full or half empty? Is the responsibility a privilege or a duty? Is the help we've been asked to give an opportunity or an obligation? Do we "get" to do it, or do we "have" to do it?

Attitude is everything. And luckily for us, our attitudes are a matter of choice. We can pick the attitudes we want much as we pick out our clothes or hairstyles. Nothing or no one in the past or present can dictate our attitudes. No one else deserves credit or blame for how we choose to process reality. For better or worse, our attitudes are ours alone.

We all have the same world to respond to. What we practice, we become. If we practice looking at each day as a new adventure, so it will be.

I will develop an attitude of gratitude each day, giving thanks for my many blessings.

April 20

Sometimes I'm awfully impressed by fools.

— Kelly Q.

The man who said this memorable line had once believed he might feel better about himself if only he owned more. As an adult child, he felt he had missed out on something and somehow got the idea he could achieve peace by acquisition. So he started to collect things like boats, expensive new cars, better clothes, and so on. His models were people who had all the toys he was now collecting. He listened to them, followed them around, and imitated them. They were his heroes.

Luckily, it didn't take him too long to discover the truth. As he got to know these people, he saw they were no happier because of what they had. One or two of them were happy, but their happiness didn't depend on what they had. The rest of them, he learned, were fools who mindlessly looked for joy and meaning outside themselves.

This man's "recovery by acquisition" experiment was only a slight detour, and he is back on the road to healthy thinking.

He is no fool.

Today, I thank God for peace and happiness and remember these riches are inside, not outside, me.

*Why beholdest thou the mote that is in
thy brother's eye, but considerest not
the beam that is in thy own eye?*
                          — *Matthew 7:2-3*

Everyone knows it's easier to look out than in.
Other people's character flaws or habits of "stinking thinking" are often as clear to us as neon handwriting on the wall. Our own kinks and dead spots
are far more difficult to identify. That difference in
"vision" is a fact: we have to accept that we tend to
be blind when we look at ourselves.

What we must not accept is the tendency to enjoy faultfinding. With practice, we can get so good
at pointing out other people's problems and clev-
erly describing them to our friends, that faultfinding becomes a skill as well as an entertainment.
Others can see our outsides as clearly as we can see
theirs. We are all glass houses. We are all vulnerable to stone-throwers.

*I will work toward always identifying an asset in
others no matter how glaring their faults.*

April 22

The endeavor, in all branches of knowledge, is to see the object as in itself it really is.
— *Matthew Arnold*

Often we can look right at something and not see it. Sometimes we see what we expect to see, sometimes we see what we want to see, and sometimes we just plain miss what's right there in front of us. If the brain and the heart aren't involved, an eyewitness account may be little better than a guess.

The acquaintance who walks right by us without a word may have lost her glasses. The attractive person we'd like to meet, while appearing conceited and aloof, may be desperately struggling with shyness and fear of rejection. The snippy salesclerk may be frantic about a teenager that didn't come home last night. Our child's sudden good grades may be the result of cheating. A tantrum may be a cry for help.

Things are not always what they appear to be. We need more than our eyes to get the picture.

I will endeavor to see beneath the surface appearance of people and events, withholding judgment until I have the facts.

*It took me years to figure out that Mom
needed the same thing I needed. Nobody gave it to her either.*

— *Patty A.*

Why go back into your family of origin? Not to
blame, certainly. And not to whitewash, either.
Useful understanding is positioned between those
two extremes. We go back to look again, as adults,
at people and events in the past. We need to understand that the care we were given — no matter
how inadequate or inappropriate — was probably
the best care they knew how to give.

Do the people we love most know how we feel?
Does our expression of that love fall short? Perhaps the people in our past had trouble bridging
the same gap. It's enlightening and often crucial to
understand the environments and systems that
taught and formed those people. Were they themselves gifted with what we so desperately wanted
them to give us? The nurturing we needed and
deserved, the holding we longed for — were they
so nurtured and held? Perhaps we didn't get it because they simply didn't have it to give.

*Evil and incapacity are not the same thing. I will
judge the people in my past as kindly as I hope
others will judge me.*

*Real joy comes not from ease or riches
or from the praise of men, but from
doing something worthwhile.*
— *W. T. Grenfell*

Joy, like happiness and freedom, is a major prize of recovery. And like these other two conditions, joy eludes those who seek it directly. It is a result of, and dependent on, something else.

Joy is a secondary effect of a primary action. When we create an environment that supports and encourages someone else, we find joy in the doing. There may be no more valuable human enterprise than lightening someone else's load, leading someone who's lost to the safe road, or extending a hand to someone who has fallen.

Such opportunities present themselves daily to recovering people. At every meeting we're in touch with people who greatly need the counsel, wisdom, and example of those who have made a decision about the past, have left behind what was, and are creating sweet new days as they walk the path of recovery.

If we hope to know joy, we must share what we have.

Today, I will pass along the kindness that has been shown me.

Recovery is . . . Being able to hang onto my own identity and have relationships, too.
— *Denise McAlister Cook*

A common characteristic of adult children is that the boundary between where others end and we start becomes blurred. Frequently we have experienced the confusion and loss of integrity that results from selling our esteem for the sake of approval — agreeing when we do not agree, laughing when we do not think the situation amusing, acting out values we do not agree with. Each time we act in this manner, our integrity slips. In time, bit by bit, it is possible to give away so much integrity that there is none left. And since our self-esteem is a direct result of the degree of integrity we have managed to retain, this sacrifice of values is of vital importance.

When I can be together with another and not lose the identity that is me, when I can care for you but still disagree, when I can say no and not become paralyzed over fear of disapproval or abandonment, then I know I am making good progress on the road to recovery.

I will examine my integrity level each day, making sure I did not diminish myself for the sake of approval.

April 26

Recovery is . . . Enjoying life more and enduring it less.
— Peggy Katherine Joseph

A young girl at a meeting announced that her mother was coming to visit a group session. Since no one knew her, one of the members asked, "How will we recognize your mother?" The girl spread out her arms and said, "By the nail holes."

It is not uncommon to find adult children with negative attitudes about life, themselves, and everyone else. More often than not, life becomes an endurance contest for people trapped in such attitudes. Such people do not see life as an adventure to be lived, but an ordeal to be survived.

Recovery shines from the faces of those who greet each day as they would the sun on a clear day. Recovering people have made the decision that life is meant to be enjoyed and they will find the joy in life in spite of the pain and disappointment that is also there. Recovery is not an exercise in delusion and denial. It is, however, a state of mind that refuses to allow these thorns in life to blot out the loveliness of the rose.

Today was given me to grow in. I will notice all the roses that line my path.

Made a searching and fearless moral in-
ventory of ourselves.
— *Step Four of* Alcoholics Anonymous

The moral inventory called for in the Fourth
Step is more like a practical accounting than it is a
listing of criminal accusations. The point of taking
the Fourth Step is to assess the facts about ourselves and how we have lived our lives. It is to pin
down the truth about who we are so we can make
better judgments about who we might become.

When we take the Fourth Step, we are looking
for recurring patterns of thought and behavior. In
searching for the story behind our story, we try to
uncover the sources of chronic trouble within ourselves. Many times, these attitudes and actions are
well concealed under layers of rationalization and
denial. It isn't easy to root them out and lay them
on the table. It isn't easy to be fearless. But it's
worth it.

The Fourth Step shines the light of truth through
the clouds of inappropriate guilt and undeserved
shame. Our willingness to face the negative also
reveals our true merits, essential goodness, and
numerous options — perhaps for the first time.

I now have enough self-worth to admit my charac-
ter flaws.

April 28

*I looked in myself so hard I lost sight of
everyone else.*

— Kim J.

Focus is important. By concentrating on ourselves, we learn to understand our patterns, rules, and consequences. That's what all this reading, sharing, and going to meetings is about. For many of us, recovery has required a look into the past to discover our roots.

However, we may become so obsessed or attached to the dysfunction of the past that looking back is all we do. Then we might spend the rest of our lives comforting our wounded child. Or we could lose sight of what is right because we too intently focus on what was wrong.

The world is filled with wonder and mystery. We are surrounded every day by many beautiful surprises: the shape of a cloud, the look in a child's eyes, the smell of fresh-baked bread, the color of the sunset, and other people — hurrying around, laughing, just plain living. We need to be aware of all the life outside and beyond us.

Today, I will look up, down, and into the faces of the other people in my world.

*The longest journey is the journey in-
wards of him who has chosen his destiny, who has started his quest.*
— *Dag Hammarskjold*

If we are not busy being born — growing, coming of age, standing up and standing out — then
we are busy dying. For that's what happens when
we consciously refuse to grow. We shrink back into
the shadows until we finally lose touch with life.

It's our fear of the shadows that makes our inner
journey so scary and so necessary. Until we dare to
face the powerful forces there — the hidden feelings of worthlessness, jealousy, fear of loneliness
— we can't gain the self-respect and confidence we
need to leave the shadows behind us forever.

Though we may be as frightened as if we were
making a planetary voyage, the discovery that our
inner universe is magnificent can only be made by
pushing on through the shadows.

*I will practice daily seeing behind my fears and
insecurities and thus discovering the beauty that is
me.*

April 30

Most of us would rather be ruined by praise than saved by criticism.
　　　　　　　　　　　— Jimmy F.

It is not always the person who tells us nice things that is our friend. Often the one who cares enough to tell us the truth — even if that truth hurts — is the one who cares the most.

Adult children oftentimes have problems with boundaries. We do not always see where we are out of bounds. We are too close to the situation. We do not have perspective. It is a friend who has some distance from us and our environment who can be more objective. When friends tell us what they see, we gain the perspective to make healthier decisions.

Just because it is criticism doesn't mean that they are right or that we should believe them. And just because it is criticism doesn't mean we should reject the person and dismiss what is said.

As I learn to accept my imperfections, I am better able to accept honesty from others.

May

*There is no such thing as "best" in the
world of individuals.*
— *Hosea Bellou*

We live in a society driven by the concept of
competition. "We are Number One" is drummed in
our ears daily via advertising and sporting events.
The message is that we must be or must have
something "better than" if we have any sense of
pride at all. Failure is the only other option.

But human behavior can't be judged according
to this kind of rating system. How could we ever
determine who is the best listener, the most in-
sightful or compassionate? At any given moment,
the best for us may not be the best for someone
else. If it goes right to the heart, a simple word
spoken at a meeting is the best word. If someone
we hardly know nods and smiles from across the
room, that smile is the best smile for us, here and
now. The extended hand, the brief word of encouragement, will never be proclaimed "Number One"
on television, never be memorialized in record
books as better than the support someone else got,
but for us, it's the best.

*I am surrounded by a multitude of blessings. I
need look no further for what I need.*

May 2

> *Life guarantees a chance — not a fair shake.*
>
> — *Bernie Y.*

Life is not fair. Most of us know that, but few of us accept it. Something in us often clings to the idea that, ultimately, the gifts will all be evenly divided. Mostly we want to be paid back for the injustices of the past. Many of us adult children expect — no, demand — redress from fate. We think life should "make it up" to us somehow. That's why it's so hard for us to go on discovering, again and again, what we already know: Life is not fair.

The good job that should have been ours, the accident that crippled a loved one, unwanted childlessness — these things are not fair. But life is like soil, not like seed. The chance of a harvest is there, but only if we plant the seed. And even then we may not get the harvest we expected or wished for — not on our own timetable. It is an act of faith, and of great courage, to keep on sowing seeds when we don't know what we're going to get. But it's the only chance we have. We need to stop expecting the soil to provide the seed.

Today, I will be grateful to be alive. This day offers a chance for a fuller life, and I will accept what comes of my efforts.

*Faith is the substance of things hoped
for, the evidence of things not seen.*
— *Hebrews 11:1*

Which comes first — the chicken or the egg, the
please or the thank you, the action or the emotion? In a recent research study, college students
were asked to make facial expressions showing
such different emotions as surprise, horror, delight, and fear. The researchers found that when
the students looked afraid, their heart rates increased and their skin temperatures dropped. They
noted similar observable reactions to the other
emotions expressed.

The implication, of course, is that even pretended emotions become "real" when they are
acted out. Action is the trigger. We are told continually in the program to "act as if." That means even
when we don't feel like smiling, acting confidently,
asking for what we need — even when such
actions seem terribly artificial — still we need to
do them. It is by doing them, by acting in faith of
what is to be, that they become real.

*I will work to understand that often my actions
need to precede my feelings if I am to make progress.*

May 4

Fear is static that prevents me from hearing myself.
                    — *Samuel Butler*

The trouble with deep feelings is they shout over the soft-spoken voices of our thoughts. When our consciousness is bombarded with the deafening volume of out-of-control emotions, perspective is impossible.

When fear is in control, fight or flight are our only options. More often than not, we choose flight and scurry off to one of our numerous hiding places. There, we can't hear the dissenting opinions voiced by our own thoughts; in effect, our most responsible self is drowned out.

But action talks louder than fear or any other rampaging emotion. If confronted directly and bravely, any tyrant emotion reveals itself as a mouse rather than a lion, a mouse whose terrifying roar is really a squeak held up to a microphone.

Let me not be intimidated by emotional outbursts. I know that persistent, rational action will see me through.

I have something important to share with you.

— *Cliff G.*

A man at a meeting asked the group if he could share a major victory in his life. When he was encouraged to do so, he cleared his throat and said quietly, "Something special happened today. The telephone book came out. And for the first time in my life, I have my name and a number listed. I'm very proud of that."

The group was silent for a moment, not knowing how to respond. Then the young man went on to explain that he was the only child of a military family — an alcoholic military family. One of his adult responses to these powerful early influences was to keep moving — physically, emotionally, and in his career. By refusing to stay put, he hoped to escape the quiet, obedient, desperate little boy inside who never knew why he couldn't make the grade.

But no more. At least not as much. No matter how much his demons pulled on his coat — he was staying put. He now has a phone, a phone number, and a listing in the book!

Recovery comes from such heroic feats.

Today, I thank my friends in the fellowship for sharing their victories as well as their defeats. Their joy is my joy.

May 6

Look not mournfully into the Past. It comes not back again. Wisely improve the Present. It is thine.
— *Henry Wadsworth Longfellow*

While our bodies go forward in time, the psyches of adult children have often stalled at some point in the past. So divided, we get confused easily by what's going on today. We're not sure what is present reality and what is merely a replay of a reality that existed twenty or thirty years ago. Recovery is learning to see the difference and being willing to do what it takes to unhook mentally and emotionally from the past.

We see this dilemma in the way we treat our children. Not only do we find ourselves lapsing into old roles, but we demand that our own children behave as we were forced to behave. We do this blindly, unknowingly, in spite of the fact that we hated such treatment when we were children. And until we take an active hand in forming who *we* are, we will continue to form our children in our own unrecovered image.

"Now" or "then" is not only our choice, it's the choice we make for our children.

Today, I pray for the wisdom to live in the present, for my children's sake as well as my own.

I pitied him in his blindness;
But can I boast, I see?
Perhaps there walks a spirit
Close by, who pities me.
— *Harry Kemp*

We have been told often enough that love is the glue that holds the world together. In one way or another we all are pursuing love as quickly and with as much creativity as we can. But love is an extremely elusive reality.

Adult children often reach for the wrong "love pot." We tend to be strongly drawn to the idea that being needed is the only way we will be accepted. If to be needed is the bottom line, we reason, then we surely must surround ourselves with those who need us. Thus we tend to become very involved with those we pity; their needs are so great.

Love and pity are not the same thing. Our love pots will not be filled by desperate people who will grasp at any help they can get.

I'm learning to tell the difference between love and pity. I am not my loved one's savior.

May 8

The only God there is, is the God above God.

— *Sister Perpetua*

At times in our quest for spiritual growth and a closer relationship with God as we understand Him, we forget that any concept, image, or belief we have of God is incomplete. No matter how great the mind that contemplates God, the image is dim indeed. A candle, to the moth that is drawn to it, may be the brightest light in the universe, but it is a dim imitation of the sun.

Our quest for God needs always to be restless. Not in the sense of frustration and a denial of serenity, but in the sense of understanding that our God is so great that the security and joy we can find in seeking God has no end. Not because we are so small, but because God is so great. A man at a meeting said he'd read that the light of stars we see in the night sky is light that started in our direction from 400,000 light years away. "All that distance," he said, "is like a marble in the hand of God. So who am I to think I can understand a Being so great as He?"

Through consistent conscious contact, the God of my understanding is more clearly revealed every day of my life.

*We, ignorant of ourselves, beg often
our own harms, which the wise powers
deny us for our good.*
— *William Shakespeare*

At times we pray fervently, trustingly, and hopefully for things that are not good for us. We are human, after all — we can see only dimly into the future, and we are often blinded by the glaring reality of our present situation.

If what we're praying for is beyond our strength or power to change, the purpose of our prayer should be to turn it over to our Higher Power rather than to get what we're asking for. Given the purest intentions and the most rigorous homework — there is much we don't and can't know. Once we've done all we can, the program teaches us to let the situation go, to let our Higher Power be responsible for the outcome.

That is the heart and soul of prayer — not to manipulate events so they come out as we think they should, but to seek the guidance and wisdom to recognize where our responsibility ends and God's begins.

I will bend my pride to the will of the Higher Power.

May 10

Think like a man of action, act like a man of thought.
— *Henri Bergson*

Anything powerful can be addicting. Anything pleasurable can be addicting. Excitement can be both pleasurable and powerful. At times, adult children engage in the most destructive activities — in relationships, finance, or family — in the pursuit of excitement.

Excitement can give us a high. It can be a substitute for the more natural highs that, if not always safe, at least have some sane boundaries. Some people have found activities like skydiving, hang gliding, or white-water rafting give them more than enough excitement without a guaranteed crash landing. Even getting excited about success, about winning, or about challenging the inner obstacles to recovery provides us with a certain excitement.

There is nothing wrong with being excited about things. The task, however, is to make sure that what we get excited about has a chance to bring us genuine celebration and is not just a shortcut to disaster.

Serenity is more important to me than any thrill or pleasure.

*Every natural fact is a symbol of some
spiritual fact.*
— *Ralph Waldo Emerson*

Our spirituality doesn't reveal itself only when
we pray, meditate, or go to church. The implications of spirituality are much wider and deeper
than that. Nearly everything we do is a reflection
of the presence or absence of a spiritual dimension
in our lives.

"How much is enough?" is a primary spiritual
question. If we are not enough, all the food, drugs,
or material goods in the world can never be
enough. A sense of worthiness is a sign of the
spirit. "Where is my security based?" is another
primary spiritual question. If my security is based
on status or the approval of the crowd, this is also
a statement about my spirituality. We act out our
spirituality when we smile and pat people on the
back or gossip and tell racist jokes.

Our spirituality defines us. We don't need to tell
anyone how spiritual we are — if they're hanging
around us, they already know.

*I seek to enrich my spirituality right now, but re-
member that it will be reflected in everything I do
today.*

May 12

> *The secret of success is consistency of purpose.*
>
> — *Disraeli*

Inconsistency is one of the biggest boulders that block our way on the road to recovery. When we're really fired up to throw off the bondage of the past, we can't wait to do what it takes. If that means meetings, then so be it. If it means reading, we will read until our eyes hurt. If it means digging into the past, just watch the cobwebs fly! For a while.

Then, sometimes much sooner than later, we figure we've done enough, the whole venture may get "old" or seem excessive — so we slack off. We don't attend as many meetings, the reading slows down, and our family of origin work is relegated to the bottom of our priority list.

The important thing is not to stop. We don't have to do it all at once, and we can't expect a high tide of enthusiasm never to ebb. We just have to do a little bit each day, no matter how we feel.

I won't let my feelings dictate how I work my program. Today, I will be consistent.

*People may doubt what I say, but they
always believe what I do.*
                                    — Ellie E.

It's maddening and frustrating when people
don't believe what we say. Not that they think
we're liars, exactly — just that they don't believe
us. When we tell them we've made a commitment,
for example, they may just roll their eyes as if to
say, "Oh sure, tell me another one."

Actions speak a lot louder than words. Before,
maybe many times before, we might have told the
same people about making the same commitment.
And then we gave it up almost as soon as we said
it. Eventually our words have no credence to anyone — including ourselves. If we want people to
believe us, we have to follow up on what we say. If
we say we won't tolerate abuse, we have to do
what it takes to stop it. If we say we are going to
take better care of ourselves, we have to make a
plan of action and stick to it. Talk is cheap.

It is amazing how quickly we can regain credibility when we walk our talk.

*Today, I will be aware of talking a better game
than I play. I will not say a thing today that I can't
back up with action.*

May 14

Works of art are indeed always products of having been in danger, of having gone to the very end in an experience, to where man can go no further.
— Rainer Maria Rilke

Given enough pressure and heat, common graphite turns into diamonds. But the process occurs only if the conditions are right, and only over time. The recovery process is something like that — certain conditions must be met over a period of time.

There's more to the process than going to meetings, even if the meetings are weekly. There are no instant transformations, no slapdash short-cuts — not if you want to end up with the real thing.

Making a free and happy life is a work of art. Writers write every day of their lives. Artists are never very far from their craft. Our task is not so different. Scant effort produces a scant result. If we want something beautiful, we'll have to give the recovery process the consistent, daily attention that brings beauty into being. And if the process involves some heat and pressure, then so it must be. Diamonds don't come cheap.

I will expect only a day's progress from a day's work.

*Loneliness is the first thing which God's
eye nam'd not good.*
— *John Milton*

Loneliness is a dominant fact of life for many people. It is also a consequence — it is caused. Regardless of the reasons behind our feelings and actions of loneliness and withdrawal, no matter how valid and compelling those reasons may be, if we give the loneliness ball a push, it's going to start rolling. If we withdraw from company or make it difficult for people to get to know us, that behavior will cause loneliness. If we habitually wear an aloof, unapproachable expression, we will not be approached. What we do (or don't do) determines what we get. And like any habit, behaviors which serve to isolate us come to feel normal, even inevitable, over time.

As long as we're alive, we're capable of building bridges between ourselves and others. Chronic loneliness doesn't have to be a fact of life. If we're willing to work at it, we can learn to reach out, make contact, and be comfortable in the company of our fellows.

Today, I will be the first to greet others and say a kind word.

> *Sometimes I'd catch my mother look-*
> *ing at me with real love in her eyes.*
> *How could she have let me down so?*
> — *Mickey C.*

For drinking alcoholics, love is incomprehensi-
ble. That word, that concept, may be just one
more thing that burdens, baffles, and frightens.
Drinking alcoholics may be willing to give us the
moon, but they simply are not able.

The adult alcoholics in our childhood probably
loved us. Maybe the clumsy cuff on the head or
the sidelong look of affection was the only expression of love they had. And maybe their bag of
tricks was completely empty. Maybe that was why
we got silence when we so badly needed affirmation. Maybe the disease, not disinterest, was behind remarks like "You could have done better" or
"I don't have time to go to your ballgame."

Many people who feel love can't act love. They
just don't have the skills to function in healthy
relationships. Their diseases or compulsions often
block the healthy relationships so desperately
needed by their loved ones and by themselves.
Possibly, we as children received everything they
had to give.

I pray for the courage to make peace with the past.
Today, I will ask for the understanding that pre-
cedes forgiveness.

As life is action and passion, it is required of man that he should share the action and passion of his time at peril of being judged not to have lived.
— *Oliver Wendell Holmes*

America's greatest killer is . . . what? Car wrecks? Heart attacks? Cancer? Alcoholism? How about suffocation by a sense of inferiority? Many of us adult children have tragic personal insight into the number of alcoholic deaths that are attributed to pneumonia, congestive heart failure, or anything but alcoholism. But feelings of inferiority are just as lethal as any of these. Although they may not appear so, people who feel a deep sense of inferiority are not fully alive.

But there is ample evidence that people do love us, that we are missed when we are not around. For all the doom and gloom that may be familiar to us aren't we surrounded also by beauty? Doesn't the sun rise each day? And don't we have it within our power to make of this day whatever we choose?

Today, I remind myself I have something to contribute.

May 18

*Because I make a mistake doesn't mean
that I am a mistake.*
— *Val B.*

Mistakes are human, and everyone makes them. There's nothing shameful about it. But maybe someone in the past taught us that mistakes were not allowed. Perhaps we learned that mistakes would cost us acceptance and approval. Looking good became everything because looking bad had such a terrible price tag. But looking good isn't the same as being good or even the same as feeling good. So, under the stress of an impossible task, many of us became our own harshest critics. We learned to reject ourselves.

But now we know we could never have learned to get up if we hadn't first admitted we'd fallen down. We know our poor judgment in the past has taught us to set healthier boundaries. And making poor choices certainly taught us what we don't want. Probably no life experience is more profitable than learning from our mistakes. In accepting our mistakes, we accept ourselves.

Today, I will look at my mistakes with both compassion and honesty. I realize my mistakes are human and are not grounds for rejection — by myself or by anybody else.

There is no grief which time does not lessen and soften.
                              — Edmund Spenser

Some stages of grief can be very confusing. Painful memories and thoughts may interrupt happy recollections. Contradictory feelings of guilt and rage may come and go — or meet each other head on. Almost anything can trigger thoughts of the person who died.

Grieving people often feel angry at everyone around them, including the doctors, themselves, and the person who has deserted them by dying. Then they may feel guilty for being angry. There may be crushing regret about harsh words or years of silence: "If only I had . . . ," or "I'm being punished because . . ." are common, if mistaken, sentiments.

Finally, though, the exhaustion lifts and the turmoil subsides. The acceptance that develops does not mean that the loved one is forgotten — it means that the death is accepted as an actual fact, a final fact. It means that we have healed enough to go on with our own lives.

I realize that the healing process takes time. I accept that my life will be changed by my loss, but that it is still my life.

May 20

A great many people think they are thinking when they are merely rearranging their prejudices.
— *William James*

We adult children may harbor deep, destructive prejudices — not against people of other colors or faiths, but against ourselves. We imagine that we know all about the limits of our abilities, the irredeemable nature of our true character, and the odds against our recovery. Like all prejudices, these "certainties" are based on ignorance and lack of reflection.

Real thinking confronts ignorance and challenges preconceived opinions. "Who says?" and "What's the basis of that idea?" are questions that thinkers ask. "I just know" and "That's what they always told me" are answers thinkers won't accept. Under thoughtful examination, the evidence we've held against ourselves often proves to be 99 percent hearsay — flimsy and insubstantial. We are not who our prejudices say we are.

Freedom lies beyond old ideas and boundaries. As we push on, we go further and faster if we leave our prejudices behind.

I am who I am today. I refuse to be burdened by yesterday's ideas.

*A relationship can't be healthier than
the people in it.*
— *Mary Kay W.*

We all dream of having marvelous relationships.
But unless we're willing to work our own recovery
program, that dream will stay a dream. The other
person in the relationship, the partner, complicates
the equation even more because he or she also
must be serious about personal growth if our
dream is to come true.

The issues faced by adult children invariably affect relationships. Why? Because it is precisely our
capacity for intimacy that has been "dented" most
as shown in our fear of commitment and in our
compulsive need to please, to never be alone, and
to place others first. We fear abandonment and are
afraid to ask that our needs be met. Intimacy is a
key relationship issue for adult children.

The first step in making our dreams come true
has nothing to do with him or her or them. It has
to do with us and our taking responsibility for our
own health and well-being.

*Today, I pray for greater understanding of my own
strengths and weaknesses as a partner in a relationship. I will make myself ready for the kind of relationship I dream about.*

May 22

This is one of those cases in which the imagination is baffled by the facts.
— *Winston Churchill*

Expectations often exceed reality. Excited children can hardly wait for their birthday parties — just the thought of the ice cream and cake, the games and prizes, the gifts, is almost too much to bear. The parents' expectations of the same event, probably focused on the preparation, the noise, and the mess, are also hard to bear — for different reasons. In neither case is the event itself half as vivid as the expectation.

Expectations color events. In fact, our expectation of what's going to happen can have a more powerful effect than anything that does happen. If we expect that an evening out will be boring, the evening will fall flat for us no matter how much fun the other people have. If we expect that the new people we meet aren't going to like us, they won't — because we won't even give them a chance to know us.

Most of us are responsible for the rain that falls on our parades. We need to lighten up, to back off, and to be more open to happy surprises.

Today, I will let go of outcomes, whether real or imagined. I will expect nothing and hope for everything.

Will is the pimp of appetite.
> — *Lope de Vega*

"Self-will run riot" is a phrase often used to describe the kind of stubborn, single-minded ferocity we sometimes substitute for problem management. Rather than back off and rethink a problem, rather than talk it over with a friend or pray for guidance, we sometimes try to force a solution by sheer, brute force of will. If an 80 percent effort doesn't do it, we rev up to 110 percent. If six hard pushes don't do it, maybe 60 will — so we keep on pushing.

More often than not, unfortunately, we focus this awesome intensity on problems that we can't change, like the ways in which other people choose to run their lives, rather than on problems we can change, like losing weight or quitting smoking. We waste enormous amounts of energy, and risk injury, by trying to coax or bully other people into doing what we want them to do. And worse — the business of living our own lives goes unattended while we're minding the business of others.

Today, I will hope for everything, but expect nothing from the people I love. I will insist on progress from myself only.

I spent twenty years before someone told me I could cut my losses.
— *Michael K.*

If we were thinking about spending a huge amount of money on a big house, you can bet we'd check first to see if the roof leaked or the basement flooded. We tend to be very careful about making major investments — and with good reason. Most of us just can't afford to make a big mistake. Why, then, do so many of us jump so carelessly into relationships?

Before committing ourselves to a large emotional investment, we can examine the total "package." We have every right to look very closely at a prospective relationship, to check it out, and to make a clear-eyed determination. Is the big draw that they "need" us? Beware. Is the person free, in fact, to make a relationship? Can the person function as a responsible adult? Is the person as committed to personal growth as we are?

If the relationship is healthy and growth-oriented, we need hesitate no longer. We can enter it knowing our optimism comes from positive, not negative, motives.

Today, I will think about my time and energy as my "capital." I will ask my Higher Power to help me spend it wisely.

Learning to trust is one of life's most difficult tasks.
— *Isaac Watts*

We are only as healthy as we are able to trust. An inability to trust, sentences us to walled-up lives protected from the deceit of others. Such isolated living makes full, human recovery impossible.

The task, however, is not to blindly trust. We have done that — to our undoing. The task is to discern who is trustworthy and who is not. Trusting has never led us into trouble, but the people we have chosen to trust have. And then all too often we have demanded unshakable loyalty from ourselves toward that untrustworthy person.

Trust must be earned. Our discipline is not to blindly trust others but to patiently wait to see if they have earned that treasured gift from us. Our goal must be to wisely discern who is trustworthy and who is not.

I am learning to trust myself as I grow in emotional stability. As I learn to trust myself, I am better able to determine when and when not to place my trust in others.

May 26

Fate chooses our relatives.
We choose our friends.
— *Jacques Bossuet*

Dealing with family of origin issues is often extremely painful for recovering adult children. All of us want to be accepted and loved by our own biological families. Some of our deepest wishes and favorite fantasies feature ourselves as loved and loving members of some healthy, whole, all-American family system. All too often that was not and is not the case. If we have to accept that, then so be it.

That's the time we should acknowledge that our real families are made up of the people who love us, whether they are relatives or not. Rather than mourn for what isn't, when family times roll around, we have the option to connect with the spiritual, functioning "family" of loved ones who want and need us to celebrate with them. The program is filled with people who will love us if we let them.

No recovering person need ever be without a family; like hearts bind tighter than like genes.

Today, I am grateful for the healing presence of my friends.

*In dealing with other people remember
the three C's: You didn't cause it, you
can't control it, and you can't cure it.*
— *Lorna P.*

None of us lives in a vacuum. We all live in relational networks called systems. There are family systems, work systems, church systems. We are constantly surrounded by and interacting with others. Some of those "others" have problems. Some of those closest to us have problems.

Adult children often display an exaggerated sense of responsibility — as if they're responsible for those problems getting solved. With this in mind we set out to "fix" the other.

The fact is we didn't cause those problems nor can we control the problems of another, and we surely can't cure them.

Recovery is an intensely personal matter — for us and for others. They will deal with their problems when they are ready, and work as hard as they choose to overcome the problems they face.

Today, I will allow others the dignity of living as they wish to live.

May 28

Admitted to God, to ourselves, and to another human being the exact nature of our wrongs.
— *Step Five* of Alcoholics Anonymous

This is the first of the Twelve Steps that necessarily involve another person. In this Step we face up and own up in order to unburden ourselves. We hand over what was, to make room for what can be. "Taking a Fifth" has far more to do with finding peace within than it does with looking for absolution outside.

First, we admit to God. The reason is that our whole program is based on honest, conscious contact with the God we understand. We admit to ourselves because our peace of mind hinges on freedom from delusion and denial. We admit to another human being because we, too, are human. In the compassionate company of another we find that in spite of all our faults and failings, we are nonetheless acceptable, lovable, and worthy. Intimate, human acceptance is based on intimate, human contact.

Is the Fifth Step easy or comfortable? Often it's not. Necessary? No doubt about it. Rewarding? It's a key to recovery.

Sharing the truth has given me a peaceful heart.

*I was acting out my patterns when I
denied that I had any patterns.*
— Julie F.

Even when we are most out of control, there is
always logic operating in our lives. B follows A,
and D comes after C. The logical pattern doesn't
cease to exist just because we're not aware of it.

This is how it works: We learned to meet our
needs in ways that were modeled for us. Some of
us learned to apologize, to play dumb, to manipulate, to rant and rave, to deny ourselves legitimate
pleasure, or to lust after those things and people
that would only cause us pain. That's A.

What we practiced we became, and what we
became stayed with us. That's B and C. There are
totally logical reasons for doing what we do and
for thinking the way we think. That's D.

Logic isn't lacking. What the logic is based on is
what causes us problems. What we learned to
practice may very well not be working. But why
we continue to practice makes all the sense in the
world.

*Today, I pray for the wisdom to recognize my pat-
terns. I ask my Higher Power to deliver me from
confusion.*

May 30

The sweet remembrance of the just
Shall flourish when he sleeps in dust.
— Nahum Tate

Memorial Day is a time for solemn reflection on those who gave the ultimate gift — life itself — for our freedom. Depending on our own or our loved ones' wartime experiences, this day comes and goes with much or little observance.

Recovering adult children can find meaning in this day by thinking of those who have gone before them — both those who died without knowing that recovery was possible and those who paid dearly for the opportunities we now have. The meetings we attend were started somewhere by someone who was, no doubt, hesitant and uncertain. The first people who identified themselves as adult children and struggled to tell their story may or may not still be alive. Most certainly they are little remembered, if they were ever known at all.

We have many blessings available to us today because someone was willing to pay the price yesterday. Let us gratefully remember those who cleared the path that we now walk.

Today, I feel at one with all adult children. I am grateful for the opportunities they created for me.

*This above all: To thine own self be
true.*
— *William Shakespeare*

Perhaps more than any other common trait,
adult children exhibit the fear of living their own
truth. After all, we may have lived most of our
lives in the pursuit of pleasing or, at least, of pla-
cating others. We hoped this would buy us the
acceptance we coveted. How could we have known
that people pleasing would strip us of our own
opinions and feelings? We didn't know we'd lose
our sense of humor, our principles, or perhaps
even our morals. We lost our own truth.

Recovery means finding it. If a joke is funny, we
laugh. If it is not, we don't. If someone else's statement is offensive, we can confront it or leave. If an
unpopular decision has to be made, we are free to
make it and go on to something else. We don't have
to please! We learn to believe our own truth as we
live it, not the other way around. Being who we
are makes us who we are. If we're not sure who we
are, today is the best of all days to start finding
out.

*Today, I will not fake my reactions to anyone or
anything. If I don't know how I feel, I will withhold my reaction until I figure it out.*

June

Friendship is a sheltering tree.
— Samuel Taylor Coleridge

Some people claim they don't want or need friends. They may say that friendship is more trouble than it's worth. They may even go out of their way to offend the people around them to make sure that there are no friendly feelings. And they usually get what they insist on — separation, distance, loneliness.

Why would anyone take that position? Almost always because there has been hurt or betrayal in past friendships. Having trusted the untrustworthy, they're no longer willing to take a chance. They won't reach out and they won't let anyone else reach in; they simply withdraw.

Once burned, it takes a mountain of courage to try again for friendship. The palms may sweat and the mouth go dry as the first hesitant contact is ventured. But the reward for repeated effort is a treasure beyond price — another human being you can care about, celebrate with, and count on, a chosen companion to keep you company along the way.

I acknowledge my need for closeness with others.

June 2

Any man's death diminishes me, be-
cause I am involved in mankind.
Therefore never send to know for
whom the bell tolls. It tolls for thee.
— *John Donne*

One benefit that can emerge from suffering is a deepening compassion. To the extent we have felt hurt and terror, we are more able to reach out to someone else in pain.

Adult children have suffered. We have walked the roads of loneliness and abandonment. To that extent we are empowered beyond others to aid in the healing of others.

We are part of mankind. We know there are countless others born and raised in dysfunctional homes. More people than we can imagine are around us seeking understanding, help, and wisdom. We are part of the universal whole. If we so choose we can take that which has caused pain and suffering and turn it into an enormously powerful balm to heal.

Today, I will reach out to anyone who needs it. I will count it my privilege to help the kind of hurt I know so well.

My spirituality has become more im-
portant to me than anything.
                              — Les G.

We like everybody to know they can count on us
to take care of things. Something needs doing on
time? Someone is needed to go the extra mile? Ask
us. For both better and worse, most of us have
learned to be the epitome of responsibility when it
comes to our jobs, children, appearance, or social
commitments.

But when it comes to taking care of ourselves
spiritually, we usually don't rate so high. Yet nothing else should be so high on our list. It is from our
spirituality that friendship and love spring up like
flowers. It is from the depth of our spirituality that
we become more able to forgive. And it is the
quality of our spirituality that determines how
well we can accept reality and let go of what needs
to be released.

Spirituality is not a luxury to be pursued only if
we have time left after we strike everything else off
the list. Quiet time, time with friends, time to
read, pray, and walk in the woods — these are all
important in the proper care of our spiritual lives.
We must beware of being too busy!

Today, I will begin to develop quiet time as a daily
habit.

June 4

A tomb now suffices him for whom the
whole world was not sufficient.
  — Epitaph of Alexander the Great

The inscription on a tomb often characterizes
the life of the person buried there. What might our
epitaphs read?

Many of us spend most of our time, energy, and
effort on matters that aren't of great importance,
even to us. Somehow, things that should be number nineteen or twenty-seven on our lists shoot up
to the top and crowd out things that should be
number one or two. We can lose not only days but
years that way, mindless of our own priorities.

Listing our top ten priorities can be an eye-
opening experience, especially if we make another
list of where the majority of our time, energy, and
effort is actually spent. We may find that what we
thought were our priorities get little time and attention. If so, obviously some decisions are in order.

At the end of the road, how will we want our
lives to be characterized?

Each day I will examine where my time and energy
went and decide if they were spent in pursuit of the
priorities I have chosen.

If eyes were made for seeing, then
beauty is its own excuse for being.
  — Ralph Waldo Emerson

It is possible to make such grim, serious business of recovery that we forget to enjoy life. But the whole purpose of recovery is to learn to live joyously, to delight in beauty, and to experience freedom. If we work so hard at recovery that we have no time or inclination to be with friends, to laugh, to discover and revel in beauty, then we have missed the point. Some people love to take long walks — when was our last walk? Some love the theater — what was the last play we saw? Some simply love to take pictures or practice any number of hobbies — do we have any activity that we do just for the joy of it?

There doesn't have to be a serious reason for everything we do. The gift of sight has been given us that we may see; we need no reason to look for beauty other than the fact that it exists. And it does. Beauty surrounds us in bewildering variety when we look for it in the people and the world around us — and in ourselves.

My life is full of beauty, and I will open my inner eye so as not to miss the joy God has so abundantly given me.

June 6

*I made you a kite so you would have to
look up.*

— *Uncle Pete*

Friends and helpers. No matter how bleak the times, if we keep looking we can almost always find one of these human rays of sunshine. But we have to keep looking.

A man at a meeting of adult children told about just such a person in his past. It was his Uncle Pete, a man who was well aware of his nephew's heavy problems. Although he couldn't do much about the boy's unhappy situation, Uncle Pete did the one thing he could do — he built the boy a kite. As he told the story now, the nephew said that he had flown the kite once in a while, but he really hadn't liked it much.

Years later he asked his uncle why he had given him that particular gift. And the uncle answered, "I made you a kite so you would have to look up."

Chances are that in our past — and perhaps still today — there are those who try the best they can to build us a kite. They encourage us and compliment us; they tell us they care while we question their motives and doubt their sincerity. We can look for such people in our lives.

Today, I will be less guarded, less defensive, less suspicious.

*Then is then. Now is now. We must
grow to learn the difference.*
— *Katie N.*

Even as adults, we can sometimes let our parents
have a ridiculous amount of control over our lives.
A mother's chance remark can bring us to tears
with anger and frustration. A father's random lack
of consideration can stick with us for weeks, eating at us and making us miserable.

Until we realize that we have a choice about the
way we respond, our emotional well-being is entirely dependent on what someone else does. Of
course other people in our lives will continue to do
and say hurtful things sometimes — we have to
accept that people are the way they are and that
we can't change them. The only changes we can
make are in ourselves. Just as we don't have to
answer the phone every time it rings, we don't
have to react to every irritation we feel. With
enough practice, we can learn to laugh at pettiness
that at one time could have made us cry.

*I will learn to be discerning about whose remarks
to take to heart. I will often counsel myself to consider the source.*

June 8

The truth shall make you free.
— John 8:32

Some of us have been so angry for so long that we don't even know we're angry anymore. Much like the effect of prolonged hunger — over time, the perception of hungriness changes to a more generalized perception of sickness. We tend to blot out what doesn't get acknowledged or resolved. Or we translate it into something else.

Because good children didn't act out anger (or so we thought) we learned very early to turn anger into hurt. And there it may well have stayed for many years, mislabeled and unrecognized. As recovering adults, we are becoming aware that a hard core of anger is under all those layers of hurt feelings. We see now that it has come out sideways for years, bruising the people we love and damaging our relationships.

Thank God we're finally able to name the problem. Naming it is the first step to doing something about it.

I will strive to see the truth, no matter how disagreeable, and name it what it is.

I found that my circumstances couldn't improve unless I did.
— *Barney V.*

If we spend enough time with other adult children we'll eventually hear someone tell a "grass is greener" story. They'll say they are moving to another part of the country to get a new start, find a better program, or to be with healthier people. If they live on the West Coast, it's the East Coast they're heading for. If they live on the East Coast, it's the West Coast that has all the answers.

But circumstances in themselves don't change people. Unless we're willing to work on ourselves, any change in circumstances will eventually not matter at all. If we stay the same, in time our circumstances will all come to be the same. Same play, different stage.

Most of us can be dysfunctional anywhere. And we can also make a healthy turnaround anywhere. The issue is not what's around us; it's what's in us.

I pray today for rigorous honesty and the ability to see that the answer is within me, not in the circumstances around me.

June 10

Fortune and love befriend the bold.
                                    — Ovid

Passivity and patience are not the same thing. We can wait our whole lives for fortune or love to come our way, but if we don't initiate action (which means risking failure) the opportunities that pass before us daily will probably never be actualized.

Boldness is the opposite of passivity. To be bold means to choose our destination, to set our own course, and to be brave enough to correct that course if we decide it's not taking us where we want to go. To be bold is to act — not with ruthless aggression — but with determined energy. It is to reach out and move toward what we are seeking rather than waiting for it to magically materialize.

When we are able to identify our wants and needs, we become better at making choices and at plotting a personal program of growth. Learning to proceed this way takes courage and practice — and the firm conviction that we are worth the trouble.

Today, I will act, not react. This day I am a hammer, not a nail.

Life can only be understood backwards; but it must be lived forwards.
— *Soren Kierkegaard*

Nearly all of us adult children have been advised, either personally or in our reading, to do some thinking about our family history. At first, we may hesitate or even stop right there. What's the point, after all? We remember how it was. What good will it do to carry on about it now? In spite of everything, many of us have intense loyalty to our parents. Why open up old wounds? The past is gone. Why rock the boat?

But family of origin work is not about *them* — it's about us. The point is that we think about the past to better understand who we are, why we act the way we do, and where our feelings came from.

Sorting through old events has just one purpose — to help us come away with insight into who we are, and where we are.

I can allow myself to look back with compassion, understanding, and forgiveness — for my family and for myself.

June 12

*I have to remember that the people on
top of the mountain didn't fall there.*
— *Sarah T.*

One of the nicest things about meetings is hearing all the success stories — stories about standing up for ourselves in frightening situations, refusing to fall into familiar old traps, and unlocking the rusty gates of communication dividing us from the people we love.

Such victories are sweet, sometimes bittersweet. Though we always rejoice with our friends, sometimes we sigh in envy as well. When we're standing in the valley, it is human to envy those who call out from the mountaintops. It is easy to forget that those people didn't fall there — they climbed there. Behind the success story is always a courageous decision and a gallant action, or a whole series of actions.

What are the mountaintops in our own lives? If we want to reach them, we can. But we have to make our own decision and our own climb. Inspiration from someone else may get us started, but the success is in the climbing.

Today, I will be very honest with myself about my feelings of envy. I will look toward my own mountaintop.

There is always free cheese in a mouse-trap.

— American Proverb

The more we feed a weakness, the more food it wants. Most of us have a particular weakness. Whether it be hot fudge sundaes, expensive clothes, or fancy cars, we all have soft spots in our hearts for one thing or another. As opposed to simple preferences and tastes, our weaknesses often cost us more than we think they will — and somehow giving in rarely satisfies: more wants more.

The reason our indulgences don't work is that they're outside remedies for inside needs. Hot fudge deprivation is not the problem. Recovery teaches us that our solutions are "in here" not "out there." We feel better when we *become* better. Every fancy car in the world would not be enough. Emptiness needs fullness — not decoration.

Outside fixes will surely give us added pounds and bigger bills and troubles we don't need. But they won't give us the answers that can only be found by searching within ourselves.

I'm less willing than I used to be to pay the price for short-term gratification.

June 14

The battle, sir, is not to the strong alone; it is to the vigilant.
— Patrick Henry

When used by recovering people, the slogan "Never compromise" is not an admonition to perfection (and therefore failure), but a statement of fact about how slips occur.

No one slips a mile at a time; we slip by the inch. If we compromise just a bit on being passive, acting out a shame-based message, or opening ourselves to toxic relationships, we crack open the door to allow the possibility of retreat.

If our concentration and resolve wander, we may not catch the momentary compromise which pushes the door still further open. Soon, without ever intending it to be so, we are back in a totally compromised position. If we don't pay attention to what we're doing, what starts with an inch ends up with a mile.

Today, I am able to recognize temptations to compromise that I couldn't have identified yesterday.

Recovery is . . . looking for more than relief from pain.

— *Anonymous*

Pain is a pretty powerful motivator. If your foot is caught in a trap, you don't worry very much about whether you'll get that promotion at work — let alone about whether your hairstyle suits you. You just want out of that trap. All energies and thoughts are focused on that foot.

So it is with us when we first approach recovery. If we're really hurting, all we want to do is escape the paralyzing pain. And for starters, that's enough. Then, as we go along working a consistent program, the intense pain lessens. We find we don't have to work as hard as we did to stay comfortable. Other concerns blur our focus on recovery.

Then we have a decision to make. Shall we stay where we are, balanced between dreadful pain and basically defensive living? Or shall we set a new, higher goal, and reach for more than survival?

When the worst of the pain is under control, what then? Recovery is stretching for all that is possible.

Today, I see possibilities that I couldn't have seen yesterday.

June 16

> *You may drive out Nature with a pitch-*
> *fork, yet she will hurry back.*
> — *Horace*

Birds don't chirp because they want to please their listeners. They chirp because they're birds, and they do it whether anyone listens or not. Like them, we are what we are — many of our best qualities are results of our individual natures, and the influence of other people has little to do with it.

Jane drinks because she's an alcoholic, not because her husband is a nag. Kim is affectionate with her husband because she's affectionate with everyone she loves. Kim is a toucher and a patter — that's her nature. Kevin enjoys home building and repair projects. Kevin's family may or may not deserve or appreciate his skill — but that's not why he's doing it.

We have little power to change anyone's nature — even our own. It is a delusion to imagine that if others love us they would change or would do things the way we want them to. No one can manipulate a lion to chirp like a bird. Fundamental orientations to life are not amenable to manipulation.

As I grow in self-acceptance, I am learning to accept other people as they are.

You can't be walked on unless you're lying on the floor.
— *Sylvia L.*

A woman told her group about the problems she was having with her kids. It seems they never did what they were told, didn't go to school unless they felt like it, and were often verbally abusive. In general, they pretty much did whatever they pleased. Of course this caused their mother a great deal of pain. As an adult child, she was asking the group for direction.

One of the members who had been sitting quietly slipped in this little gem of wisdom, "You can't be walked on unless you're lying on the floor. If you don't like the footprints on your back, why don't you stand up?"

The abused parent probably didn't like to hear that, but it was the truth. At times we all tend to blame our problems with others on their stubbornness or selfishness. But the other side of that picture, the side we can do something about, has to do with passivity.

Today, I ask my Higher Power to back me up when I assert my rights. Today, I will not let myself be abused.

June 18

They may not need me, but they might.
I'll let my head be just in sight.
A smile as small as mine may be
Precisely their necessity.
— *Emily Dickinson*

All of us — old, young, crippled, fit, has-beens, never-weres, outgoing, and shy — all have gifts to give. There's no good reason amongst all the familiar excuses: "No one wants to listen to an old lady like me," "I'm really not a joiner — can I make a contribution?" "I'm too tired," "I don't have time," "I'm afraid because I've never done anything like that before."

People who join a program of service, as we have, oblige themselves to serve. If we can pick up a phone, make a pot of coffee, stack folding chairs, or just greet a newcomer by name, we can make a contribution. If we can give someone a ride, pat someone on the back, or say a friendly word, we can make a real difference. It's far more important that we do something, anything, than bow out of service altogether. There are those waiting now, today, for exactly what we have to offer.

My growing self-esteem enables me to be a participator rather than a spectator.

Speak of one that loves not wisely but too well.
— *William Shakespeare*

Smother love springs from the belief that the beloved must be catered to, controlled, or even physically clutched to be kept from leaving us. Smother love is not successful, and may encourage the loved one to leave.

Many adult children have felt lonely and abandoned. They are petrified that love will abandon them again. The desperate intensity that translates as smothering is characterized more by feelings of fear than of love. It is best for us if we understand our real motive and recognize obsession for the trap that it is.

Genuine love doesn't entrap — it lifts up and sets free. No matter how much we force, push, or contain, we cannot expect to be loved by those we would imprison.

I am increasingly less compelled to control the lives of my loved ones. I am relieved to put down a tool that has never worked.

June 20

Pain doesn't guarantee gain.
— *Marcia A.*

We are all familiar with the saying, "No pain, no gain." There is a grain of truth in that. But it is also true that we can set ourselves up for a lot of pain without gaining a thing. Of itself, pain doesn't guarantee success.

Pain never pays off, for example, when we insist on misnaming what is going on in our lives. If we call our workaholism responsibility, that cycle will never be broken. If we look at our inability to play as "devotion to serious duty," we will never learn to play. If "bad luck" is how we describe a long series of destructive relationships, there will be no end to the disappointments. Pain will beget only more pain, just as it has before.

We have to be honest about what it is that's really happening. Misnaming is a form of lying. And it guarantees that there will be no gain.

Today, I will examine the labels I've attached to my life situations. Am I telling myself the truth?

*Marriage may be compared to a cage:
the birds outside despair to get in and
those within despair to get out.*
— *Montaigne*

Marriage is surely one of the most emotionally confusing words in our language. Some of us tend to feel (if not think) that marriage is a total fraud and that "happy marriage" is a contradiction in terms. Yet there are happily married people. Some of us deeply believe that if only we were married, all our problems would be over — especially loneliness. Yet some of the loneliest people on earth are married.

Marriage, in a sense, is a condition like wealth — it's not so much if we are or aren't, but how we relate to the situation. If a marriage is healthy, it can be a mighty hedge against loneliness. But if the marriage is unhealthy, all sorts of miseries are possible.

The issue for happiness is not a question of married or not, but of our own self-esteem. If we are recovering and think well of ourselves, then we can find love, happiness, and the face of God each day — married or not.

Today, I have no unrealistic expectations of marriage. No one but me is responsible for my own fulfillment.

> *Unless I accept my virtues, I most certainly will be overwhelmed by my faults.*
>
> — *Robert G. Coleman*

For many shame-based reasons, it is always easier to acknowledge our flaws than our good features. Perhaps, in the beginning, we sought modesty over vanity when we learned to focus on imperfections. Since we didn't want to be conceited, we downplayed our good qualities until we forgot they existed. But even the best intentions can backfire.

To recover is to comprehend truth. And the truth is, there is much that is right about us. The very fact that we are thinking, reflecting, and perhaps acting on the meditations in this book says many good things about us — that we are open-minded, sincere, and willing to make an effort.

Until we accept the whole truth, our reality is based on a partial truth. Habitual self-deprecation isn't a virtue; it's a handicap that needs to be eliminated.

I am a good person, and I am becoming better every day. I will not define myself by my flaws.

*I knew other people's minds better than
I knew my own.*
                                — *Wayne W.*

She had three grown kids and no marketable skills. She was fifty and now alone. Her alcoholic husband had left her for a woman she described as young enough to be his granddaughter.

Her pain was intense and seemed to flash out of her like lightning. She wanted to stop hurting — to heal. But even more, she wanted her children to heal. Their problems had followed them into adulthood.

It would have been hard not to notice that every sentence the woman spoke began with "he." Even though he was gone and not coming back, she was still centering her life around him. All the possibilities were still being filtered through the departed ex-husband.

It is a sure sign we're moving on when we say, "Here is what I think," rather than "This is what they think"; "Here is what I feel," rather than "This is what they feel." Reality includes many things that are cruelly unfair, but freedom roots in reality and nowhere else.

I pray that I may live in the present, no matter how difficult it is. I will not filter my future through people from the past.

June 24

To be confident is to act in faith.
— *Bernard Bynion*

Confidence is a wonderful word that names a truly wonderful personal attribute. It comes from two Latin words meaning "with faith." When we have assurance and conviction about what we're doing, we have faith that we will do it well. We are confident.

Although we adult children may see ourselves as anything but models of confidence, the fact is that we are self-assured about many things. Perhaps it's a skillful tennis serve or a special recipe that never fails. Maybe it's our ability to change a flat tire in five minutes or to balance a checkbook to the last penny. We may not acknowledge our expertise or allow it to count for much, but all of us have faith in at least a few abilities.

As we recover, we gradually learn to replace self-doubt and hesitancy with a growing sense of confidence, not in just one or two areas, but in ourselves. By acting in faith, we prepare ourselves to receive the gift of faith.

I trust that by working the program I will one day be confident.

*I had to learn not to test the depths of
water, or of people, with both feet.*
— *Robbie L.*

Trusting is important. Learning to trust is a key
element in recovery. But it's equally important to
learn to trust only trustworthy people. How can
we know who is trustworthy and who is not? This
is tricky business for adult children because our
mistaken judgments in the past have blurred our
present boundaries.

Robbie's comment is a wise one. We don't
plunge in and test the depth of unknown water
with both feet. Why should we test people that
way? Trust must be earned. It must be deserved.

Before totally trusting anyone, we must think
about what is important to us, what we really
want in a friend or partner, and what our boundaries are. Are they faithful to us? If so, it is probably
safe to trust a bit more. Do they consistently perform in little ways? Then chances are they can be
trusted further.

We don't owe trust to anyone. We give it as a
gift.

*Today, I pray for the wisdom to give my trust only
to trustworthy people, and the insight to recognize
who they are.*

June 26

*This is the day which the Lord has
made. Let us rejoice and be glad in it.*
— *Psalms 118:24*

Value this day. Despite all our fears and uncertainties, each ordinary day is a fantastic opportunity to know more, do more, and be more. Even our most fondly remembered yesterday or vividly imagined tomorrow is far less important than the new, untried promise that today is, because today is here. We have our hands on it right now. As the saying goes, "Yesterday is a canceled check, tomorrow is an IOU, today is cash — spend it wisely."

With all its stress, traffic jams, family squabbles, or loneliness, today is precious. We need some pressure and uneasiness to keep us moving in our search for harmony. Some restlessness is necessary. When tension ends, so does life. We must resolve to find the spirit in everyday life — not in spite of it. To fall in love with today is the task of every living person who hopes for a better tomorrow.

I will embrace today and all it holds — promise, adventure, disappointment, and growth.

Were entirely ready to have God re-
move all these defects of character.
— Step Six of Alcoholics Anonymous

Readiness is the key to all important passages in
life. Until we're ready to know something, the
mystery is not revealed. Until we're ready to do
something, the power is not mobilized. Until we're
ready to receive a gift, even if we trip over it, that
gift will not be ours. It may not even be recognized
as a gift.

The Sixth Step talks about our readiness to have
the obstacles to our happiness removed. These obstacles are our character defects. Until we're ready
to let them go — boxed up, on the porch, waiting
for pickup, so to speak — they will be left with us.
It's that simple.

The Sixth Step is also very specific about who
will take them away. For all our intelligence and
willpower, we're not the ones who do the remov-
ing. When we're ready to admit the power of God
into our lives, and only then, we will be ready for
freedom.

The experience of my fellows has empowered me to
have faith in renewal.

June 28

Be not afraid of life. Believe that life is worth living and your belief will help create the fact.

— *William James*

Many adult children learn that rejection and abandonment are part and parcel of being alive. We are so used to feeling as though things won't work out, that fear — like a shadow — is always lurking behind us. Usually there's something specific to be afraid of — that we won't have enough money to pay our bills, someone we love will die, or our children won't do well in school. And always there's the generalized fear that events will overwhelm us in spite of our best efforts.

We need to be careful about creating what we look for. Regardless of the frightening experiences of the past, we need to believe that other results are possible: All loved ones don't leave, all risks don't end in devastation, and all efforts aren't dashed on the rocks of defeat.

New consequences are possible when we believe they're possible. The brave new world that each of us seeks stands on the shoulders of that belief.

I am sick and tired of being fearful. Today, I am confident that positive efforts will yield positive results.

The biggest liar was my own addiction.
— Joanie R.

We have lived with dishonesty — in others and in ourselves. Many of us had to learn to cope with the obvious lies accompanying our parents' dysfunction or the enabling of that dysfunction. One of the ways we coped was to convince ourselves that our perceptions were false. A low self-image and our own eventual dishonesty caused us pain, and some of us found momentary relief in addictions or other compulsive behaviors.

But addictions also lie. All of them — no matter to what substance or behavior — speak to us softly and seductively: "Try me, I will take away the disappointment, the loneliness, the rejection, the pain. I will heal you." The lie, of course, is that addictions help anything because even after a binge, the pain is there. And it is often worse.

Switching addictions is no good either. Switching to work, sex, food, money, religion is not a way out. Freedom from all addictions is found in truth. And the truth is we need to face our realities without addictions.

Today, I will examine my life for switched addictions. I will ask my Higher Power to help me stay on course.

June 30

*The race is not always to the swift, but
to those who keep on running.*
— *Anonymous*

Recovery is mostly a long-distance runner's game, not a sprinter's. Frequently people begin recovery and attend group meetings with an energy that staggers the imagination. They are on every committee, constantly busy about helping others, quick on giving advice. It all looks so good.

But there is a question: A year from now, or in five years, where will they be? Will they have skipped over so many of their own broken parts in a rush to heal others that shortly down the road they fall apart?

If recovery is to be likened to a race at all, it most certainly is about the plodding, patient, and humble runner who clearly knows that what is called for is to put one foot in front of the other and then do it again.

I am less interested in making a "big finish" than I used to be. I accept the fact that recovery is a long-term process.

July

*People need loving the most when they
deserve it the least.*
— *John Harrigan*

When life is flowing benevolently along and our
hands are full of aces, we need little support and
affirmation. It is when things turn mean and all
light seems to have gone from the sky that we most
need support and love — especially from ourselves.

All of us make mistakes. All of us are far from
perfect. Failures take many forms — some serious,
some repeated despite many promises that this
would not happen again. It may be something
small to others but big to us — going back on a
pledge not to binge eat or catching ourselves being
consistently negative. It may be large — walking
away from a relationship that could have worked.
When we fail is when we most need to remind
ourselves of our humanity and treat ourselves with
love.

We so often forget what works. When we have
failed, we need not take vengeance on ourselves
but, rather, find a way to regain our feet as quickly
as possible. The more loving we are to ourselves
the easier it is to get up and start again.

*Like a baby who learns to calm herself after a bad
dream, I too am learning to rely on myself for
comfort.*

July 2

> *I need to get my heart's hands off the*
> *steering wheel.*
>
> — *Warren G.*

So spoke an adult child at a meeting. The subject was feelings and the havoc they can play in our lives. Warren's point wasn't that feelings are bad, of course. And it wasn't that feelings should be repressed. The point was that feelings have to be managed — they can't run the show.

Warren said his tendency was to allow his feelings to dictate how he thought and behaved. He said that blindly following his feelings had caused him trouble — endless repetition of the same old behavior that produced bad results every time. That's when he came up with the above saying.

When we are feeling lonely, we can't let that feeling call the shots. We need to pry that feeling's hands off the steering wheel. When we feel passive and submissive, we need to refuse those feelings access to the controls so we can keep moving straight ahead with our program.

Today, I will identify two or three feelings that get me into trouble. Today, I will keep them out of the driver's seat.

*Our life always expresses the result of
our dominant thoughts.*
— Soren Kierkegaard

We need to be aware of what we think — for as we think, we are. Our minds are like extremely powerful magnets pulling the reality of our lives into place. Whatever the dominant thoughts may be, they in effect create the quality of our day-by-day living. If we allow our thoughts to be consumed with the fearful, negative, and defeatist ghosts of the past, then we have decided what our present shall be since our thoughts determine our reality.

As recovering adult children we must make decisions as to whether we will entertain thoughts of the past — no matter how vivid or persistent — or whether we will choose to think of something else. We can rise above the conditioning of the past and choose thoughts of courage, of freedom, of community. Our dominant thoughts form the outer, concrete reality of our lives.

Today, I choose to focus on the possibilities of life rather than the perils.

July 4

*Freedom is the right to choose; the right
to create for yourself the alternatives of
choice. Without the exercise of choice,
a man is not a man but a member, an
instrument, a thing.*
— *Archibald MacLeish*

Gaining personal freedom is no easy matter. Not
that it's impossible to achieve; rather, it's all too
possible, in our heart of hearts, not to really want
authentic freedom.

One of the prices of freedom is the requirement
that we name our slavery. How we dig in our heels
when it's time for such honesty! We dread it so
much we may refuse to even attempt change, let
alone accept a program of change and stick with it.
But there is no other way. We can't slip off the
chains of slavery if we refuse to see where they are!

But however deep our habits or powerful our
compulsions — there are others of us in the program who have had similar feelings. We are not
the first or the worst. If we must begin by praying
to want freedom, then that's where we begin.

*Today, I move toward greater freedom by looking
with greater understanding on my fears.*

It was the worst time of my life. I couldn't go forward and I couldn't go back.

— *Cherry F.*

Some decisions are very hard to make. But indecision is hard, too. It fixes us, in fact, right at the point of pain. Not to decide is not to go on. In the end, it causes more pain than making the hard decision.

To waffle back and forth between yes and no, stop and go, is to walk right up to the brink and then back off. Rather than trusting ourselves to do what has to be done, we fight the same battle again and again. Postponement isn't relief. Indecision isn't a solution.

Decisions about whether or not we need to make amends, whether we should get into or stay in a relationship, whether now is a good time to start that diet or stop smoking — all carry price-tags. There is probably no decision for change that isn't difficult to make. But indecision guarantees that change won't happen. With practice we can learn to trust in our ability to shape our lives.

I pray for clear insight about my own decision-making process. I pray for courage to take care of business.

July 6

Pity me that the heart is slow to learn
What the swift mind beholds at every
turn.

— *Edna St. Vincent Millay*

It's the same for all of us. Sometimes we know very well that a decision must be made long before we're emotionally ready to carry it out. Perhaps a health crisis demands a new way of life, or maybe the time has finally come to terminate a toxic relationship. Whatever the issue, the conflict is the same — the mind has decided to let go, but the heart hangs on.

We shouldn't be surprised at this phenomenon, or too disappointed in ourselves. Of course there's a lag between knowing and doing. As in all other aspects of working the program, admission comes before acceptance, rarely alongside it.

While it lasts, the conflict is painful. But it doesn't last forever. If we keep pushing toward truth, our emotions will let go of their unrealistic fantasies and harmony will be restored.

I am willing to work and wait for inner harmony. I know that it will come.

What comes from the heart touches the heart.

— *Don Sibet*

Some of the stories told at meetings of adult children are dramatic and memorable. Sometimes they're heartbreaking, sometimes they're hilarious, and sometimes they're intimidating. Why? Because we tend to confuse the talk and the talker. We tend to put ourselves down by putting other people up: "Oh, I wish I could talk like Sarah!" Or, "I didn't volunteer because I was hoping you would share!"

What hogwash! People who have an easy time putting words together don't necessarily share better than anyone else. It's not how we say it that counts — it's that we trusted enough to say anything! True sharing is venturing into vulnerability, letting some of our real self come out front so it can be healed and loved. You don't have to be a good storyteller to be a great sharer.

I will do my part to enhance my group by sharing as honestly as I can.

July 8

Recovery is . . . Spending more time building relationships than worrying about losing them.
— *Anonymous*

Recovery means walking in the sun. It means progressively living in favor of what might be rather than defending ourselves from the disasters we are sure life has in store for us.

Adult children routinely live in debilitating fear of what might happen in their relationships. We tend to spend so much time worrying about the calamity that may befall us, we find it impossible to enjoy what is there and put out the energy and time to create new, exciting connections.

Nothing is forever. Some relationships simply are not destined to be eternal. As we recover we come to understand this truth. We grow to where our self-esteem and sense of self is not based on this relationship or that one but on our ability to move with the flow of life. Recovery is being open to the possibilities of what might be.

In accepting that I can't control outcomes, I have much less fear of the future.

I accept the universe.
> — *Margaret Fuller*

To tolerate something is to put up with it even though we don't especially like it. To maintain sanity, we try to ignore or brush off annoyances like traffic noise, the co-worker who talks too much, or our children's taste in TV shows. We don't want to make big deals out of little deals and we don't want to be upset all the time. So we tell ourselves it doesn't matter — sometimes through clenched teeth.

Acceptance goes one step further than tolerance. One giant, important step. To accept something is to receive it willingly — without white knuckles or clenched teeth. Acceptance issues from the heart, not just the head. To accept an irritation is to achieve more than a stressful stand-off, or a grudging deafness or blindness to it. It is to embrace it, and thereby take away its power to intrude on our serenity.

My serenity will not be sacrificed to the annoyances of daily life. I will take my world as it is.

July 10

My program isn't overwhelming — my expectations are.

— Rita Z.

Sometimes it all seems like too much. The enormous changes we need to make seem simply overwhelming. The road is too long, too steep, too rocky. We sometimes feel like we'll never make it.

We can sabotage our recovery with that kind of thinking, because it's not the case at all. We're not making the whole trip today. Baby-step-by-baby-step is the way we go. Recovery doesn't require us to become totally new people overnight. It does ask us to begin somewhere, anywhere, and do what we can.

Whatever we can do is just what we should be doing right now. If that means reading just one sentence a day — great! If it means sharing just one small truth with a friend — it's a start, a beginning step down the road.

Even monumental change is often a gradual occurrence. We don't see how great the change has been until we walk the road a while. Then, looking back, we see how far we have come. We must not expect too much too quickly.

Today, I pray for patience and perseverance. Today I will not be my own bogeyman.

Wisdom arises from the sharing of concerned, intelligent people.
— *Rev. Bob McClendon*

Most meetings circulate a phone list. The people who have put their telephone numbers there want us to call them. An important part of working their program is "giving it away to keep it." The point is they need us as badly as we need them; the help goes both ways.

Why call? Because these are sharing, caring, supportive people, people who will say, "You don't have to go it alone unless you choose to. Please don't. We can't choose for you, but we want you to know we understand, we love you, and we are here."

As hard as it is for most of us to start using that phone list, it is a vital element in our support system. If we need to talk, we shouldn't hesitate to pick up the phone.

I will use my group's roster list, understanding the one I call may need to share with me as badly as I need to share.

> *Being alone is a markedly different experience than being lonely.*
> — *Clark E. Moustakas*

Being left alone is just about the most crushing, terrifying eventuality that many of us can think of. Past experience has taught us to equate aloneness with abandonment, if not punishment. So we do whatever we have to do to avoid separation from the group. If no one else is handy, we'll settle for a face on TV or a voice on the radio — anything but our own company.

Yet we run from opportunity when we run from solitude. Understandable as our fear of aloneness may be, it is only in quiet solitude that we can see with the spirit. Only in stillness can we come face to face with our own beauty and truth.

It may indeed take practice and no small amount of courage, but we can learn to love solitude. If we become willing to spend time with our own best friend — ourselves — we need never be lonely again.

I will spend some quiet time with myself today. I can learn not to be afraid of my own company.

I never realized how often I used the words "just" and "only."
— *Mary Pat K.*

Adult children often live within a framework of shame. One symptom of this is we minimize our achievements, feelings, needs, or opinions. Behind that is our feeling that we aren't and can't do anything special. So it figures we would find a way to discount whatever we do.

Two words we use frequently are "just" and "only." We say things like, "Our house has only two bedrooms" or "I only got a red ribbon at the state fair, and my tomatoes didn't place" or "I'll just eat these leftovers for dinner, and you can have the steak."

These are ways of saying, "I don't count."

But, of course, we do *count*. How freeing it is to grow to the place where we say, "I've only entered the state fair once and I won a ribbon. I'm proud of myself." Or, "No, I don't want the leftovers either. Let's share the steak."

We give strength to minimizing attitudes when we use minimizing words. We deserve better.

Today, I will not minimize my achievements or needs. I will give someone an honest opinion about an issue that matters to me.

> *The closest to perfection a person ever*
> *comes is when he fills out a job applica-*
> *tion form.*
> — *Stanley J. Randall*

If it weren't for the Joneses, maybe we wouldn't judge ourselves so harshly. We wouldn't try so hard if they weren't perfect spouses, parents, and members of the community. But perfection is how we see the Joneses, and that imaginary perfection is the standard by which we measure ourselves.

Obviously, the Joneses have to be dealt with. They drive us all crazy. Who needs the discouragement, the intimidation, the exhausting chase? The problem is that the Joneses don't live in the real world, but in our minds. They're the idols we create in order to hate; the impossible images we use for a variety of personal, perverse reasons, to reinforce our sense of inadequacy.

There are no real Joneses, of course. The perfection we imagine in other people is about as real as the ghost that is nothing but a sheet on a stick. "Why can't we be like the Joneses?" isn't the question. "Why do I need to fantasize the Joneses?" is what needs answering.

Today, I will judge my progress according to my own standards. I will run my own race and sing my own song.

When men are easy in their circumstances, they are naturally enemies to innovations.

— *Joseph Addison*

We are all born into an existing pattern and then create our own network of relationships. One important rule of a system is that it stay stable. Even depressed family systems generate enormous energy to maintain the status quo. Even the weakest, sickest systems resist change.

Since recovery means change, we shake up our family systems when we dare do something different. Why? Because our rocking the boat threatens the whole system. In order to protect itself, our family system may very well not celebrate and support our change — no matter how good it is for *us.* It may, in fact, try to stifle the change we are campaigning for.

Recognizing this dynamic can help us understand why the people closest to us may be our biggest obstacle to continued growth. Until new stability is gained, over-reaction is to be expected. The old system is just protecting itself.

I am willing to risk temporary discomfort for the rewards of a better life.

July 16

*Enablers are the worst enemies of the
very people they love the most.*
— *Carrie R.*

Enablers are those of us who take the responsibility to protect other people from pain. If someone near us feels down or unhappy, we believe it is our job to make them feel better.

Despite our good intentions, our enabling has a negative side: In protecting others from pain, we also shield them from a marvelous teacher and motivator — experience. We prevent them from taking responsibility and from living with the consequences of their decisions. When enablers, even motivated by love, gallop onto the scene, they deprive their loved ones of the motivation they might need to make some changes.

Recovery requires change, and change often begins with a conversion experience. Conversion experiences can be rooted in pain. If we enablers are always there to cushion the fall, how are our loved ones going to meet the concrete? Our own growth might be due to those who loved us enough to let us experience the painful consequences of our mistakes. We can pass this loving detachment on to others.

Today, I will allow others to live with their own choices.

*The children of this world are in their
generation wiser than the children of
light.*

— Luke 16:8

When we think of our child within, many of us
sense only the wounded child — the child who
feels afraid, inadequate, needy, and shut out. It is
true of course that we all have a child within. But
that child is wise and strong, as well as wounded.

Beneath the fears and doubts, deeper than the
guilt and shame, our inner child knows some
truths that our adult selves aren't always sure of.
That child, like all children, wants to imagine and
play, to unconditionally love and be loved, to find
out what's really important and to care about it.
Even if the child was not allowed to act out those
wants, the wants remain, stored away. Our child
within still wants, craves, and reaches out for the
eternal truths of successful living. We need to pay
heed to our child's sense of wisdom and trust, as
well as to give that child within us our adult capacity for sympathy and comfort.

*I can allow myself a childlike wonder and curios-
ity. I will look at the world today with new eyes.*

July 18

*Meditation is a mental discipline that
enables us to do one thing at a time.*
— Max Picard

The logic is simple enough: If your plate is full,
stop piling on more. When we consistently have
too many things to think about and do, we can
become ragged and dysfunctional. When we get in
that spot, what helps is to pull back from all of it
and allow but a single thought. It may be the loving face of someone dear to us. It may be a nature
scene that we have enjoyed — a mountain view or
a beach, a bunch of spring flowers or a waterfall.

As we develop the mental discipline to focus on
a single thought, we become able to hold it for
minutes instead of seconds. And when our time of
quiet contemplation is over, we find that our lists
and our schedules have not devoured us after all,
and that we are better able to deal with our projects — if we take them on one at a time.

*I will become aware of wasting my energy by deal-
ing with too many things at one time.*

When I am on the move my God is
with me.

— *Ross B.*

God is much more a verb than a noun. Verbs are
action words. They name an energy, a movement,
a happening. Nouns are solid and static, they don't
move. God is more a force than a monument. To
think of God as a verb is to discover a meaningful
dimension of that relationship. "Up there" or "in
here" doesn't by any means tell the whole story of
what goes on between us and our Higher Power.

As we travel the road to recovery, our Higher
Power is always moving with us. This is the energy
that travels with us from where we are to where we
are going, from what is to what can be, from good
to better, better to best.

Our lives are always in process, moving, changing. To begin to see our Higher Power in that way
is to recognize the Power behind our power and
the Thought behind our thoughts. God is the juice,
the energy, that moves us from death to life.

We don't travel alone.

Today, I will meditate on the difference between
the God I knew as a child and the God I am now
discovering. I will be grateful for maturity.

> *The price of greatness is responsibility.*
> — *Winston Churchill*

Maybe a relative will leave us a lot of money. Maybe someone will have done the ironing by the time we get home from work. Maybe we'll suddenly decide that we don't like chocolate anymore. Maybe. Wonderful things do happen by accident once in a while — but we would be pretty foolish to sit back and wait for our lives to be validated by an accident.

Recovery is far too important to leave to chance. If we don't change the old habits, rules, and attitudes, they won't be changed. And if we don't do enough work on our family of origin, we probably won't be able to identify just what those habits, rules, and attitudes are and where they came from. Unfortunately, that information never just falls into our lap; we don't find it by accident.

Our lives won't be ruined if we don't get an inheritance or if we have to do our own ironing. That kind of wishing is harmless and even fun. Wishing for recovery is another matter entirely.

I will not confuse daydreams with footwork. I know that my recovery depends on me.

Great deeds are usually wrought at great risks.

— *Herodotus*

Everyone at the meeting could identify with Nancy. She was talking about her strange and surprising reaction to the divorce she was going through — a divorce that she initiated after much thought, prayer, and counseling. In her mind, Nancy was convinced that the divorce was necessary as well as long overdue. Emotionally, however, Nancy said she felt frantic to the point of calling the whole thing off.

Some other members who had walked the same path assured her that her reaction was anything but surprising. For us adult children, they explained, letting go — even of something dreadful — means being at risk. Since our emotions can't tolerate that, they tend to hang on, even to toxic relationships that are slowly killing us. Just wait, they promised Nancy, what is ahead will be better than what was behind. Life is worth the risk.

Today, I will investigate which of the patterns in my life are negative, and I will think about ways to change them.

July 22

*Forgive all who have offended you, not
for them, but for yourself.*
— *Harriet Uts Nelson*

We adult children could make long lists of legitimate complaints against those who have offended us. Without exaggeration or dramatization, some of the misdeeds that we've endured are horrendous, even unforgivable in the popular sense of the word. But are they really unforgivable?

Even though we have been denied what is essential and have been force-fed that which destroys, we must think long and hard about the consequences of withholding forgiveness. Even though holding an eternal grudge seems not only emotionally necessary but reasonable, we need to realize that harboring resentment makes us — again — victims.

Forgiveness is in our own self-interest. Refusal can chain us forever to the hideous situation we won't let go of. We can't get free until we forgive.

What's done is done! When I forgive someone I don't let anybody off the hook but myself.

There is no such thing as "all at once" in recovery.

— Bill S.

The journey of recovery is unique. Unlike other journeys, we can't just pick a destination, hop a jet, and get there quickly on the power of the plane. We are the mode of transportation and the territory to be covered on the recovery journey. We are the ticket agent, the pilot, and the navigator. The program is the map — but the rest of the journey is up to us.

It's unrealistic to expect a quick or smooth journey. And unrealistic expectations generate discouragement, which makes us want to quit. Inexperienced as we are, we have to remember that, as we start out, we simply don't have all the skills we need to make the journey. We get them as we go, often one at a time, one day at a time. If our progress seems slow, then fine. The *Santa Maria* was slow, too, but it got there.

I will learn to be patient with my rate of progress accepting all movement onward as a major success.

> *Once to every man and nation comes*
> *the moment to decide . . .*
> *And the choice goes by forever 'twixt*
> *that darkness and that light.*
> — *James Russell Lowell*

At conventions of recovering adult children, hundreds of healing, growing people come together to celebrate, share their experiences, and renew each other's strength. Behind every marvelous tale of death-left-behind is a common theme of peak moments — moments of rare awareness and maximum readiness. Each story tells of a moment of truth which became a time of decision.

No one can say that we have only one such moment, or one such chance. Perhaps there are many pivotal opportunities, but only a few that find us prepared. Perhaps we will never run out of chances to make the decisions that lead to recovery; these peak moments may occur as long as we live.

Or they may not. It may be that, in some mysterious economy, our chances are numbered. Squandered readiness may be lost forever. Perhaps we'd better make our decisions some day sooner than tomorrow.

I recognize that any day can be a great day if I choose to make it so.

Next year I'm going to be better than I am now, but today I'm the best Jeanie I can be.

— *Jeanie F.*

It is quite possible to waste a lot of time and energy trying to make impossible changes. Many of us, inspired by the dynamics of the program and driven more by enthusiasm than prudence, strike out on missions that cannot be accomplished. Missions we cannot win and should never undertake.

Turning back the clock is one of these. It can't be done. Controlling someone else's behavior is another. We can set the stage for the desired behavior, encourage it, and improve the odds by getting out of the way — but we don't have it in our bag of tricks to *make* people think, feel, or do any one thing.

The program addresses *the art of the possible*. The only options we have are the options that are available to us. If our former partners don't *want* to reconcile with us, that's not an available option. A happily-ever-after marriage is not possible if we have yet to learn how to have a healthy relationship. Instead, we can focus on acquiring these people skills by building on our own possibilities.

Today, I will examine my range of available choices.

July 26

Humility is truth.

— *Erasmus*

Try to build a house from a haphazard blue-print, and the result will be a disaster. Use inaccurate data to guide your investments and you'll end up broke. Solid progress can only ensue from a solid, accurate starting point. This is true in any field of human endeavor, and it is certainly true of personal growth.

Humility is truth. As such, humility is essential to any program of recovery. It is our solid starting point, the X on the map that tells us where we are as we start our journey. The state of spirit we call humility has the power to take us beyond delusion and denial. To gain humility is to go far beyond owning our faults. We must also learn to own the reality that we are good people, people who try and who make mistakes in the pursuit of accept-ance and love. Humility is not about breast-beating and self-accusation; it is about recognizing the truth and accepting it.

Today, I will reevaluate my ideas about humility. I will not be afraid to see myself as I am.

Work, and thou wilt bless the day
Ere the toil be done;
They that work not, cannot pray,
Cannot feel the sun.
　　　　　— John Sullivan Dwight

Confusion is often a cop-out. Usually we know very well what needs to be done about our lives and we even know how to do it. As they say, "Working a program is simple . . . but it ain't easy." If we are honest, we have to admit that "What am I supposed to do?" isn't the real question at all.

Any young athlete knows how to work a program: practice times are not to be missed, after-school entertainments are given up, and new techniques are drilled again and again until they are natural. Students, too, work their program by sitting down with their books no matter how they feel. They practice good study habits until they have good study habits.

Achieving a new way of life consists of conscientiously repeating positive actions — nothing confusing or mysterious about it. We must be willing to exercise the discipline if we want to reap the rewards of a healthy lifestyle.

Today, I will welcome the patterns that lead to success.

Humbly asked Him to remove our shortcomings.

— *Step Seven of*
Alcoholics Anonymous

Step Seven builds on the readiness for recovery we achieved in Step Six. It not only tells us what to do next, it names the attitude we must take in doing it.

We are told specifically that we must ask. There is no implication that we should think it over, wish for it, or make another attempt to haul the garbage ourselves. It says we are to ask God to do this. And it says we are to ask humbly. We don't make demands or strike bargains with God. God doesn't bargain.

Humility isn't self-abasement; humility is truth. A humble attitude is simply one that recognizes where our power ends and God's begins. The humble request of the Seventh Step means we have made an inventory, bundled up our discards, and called for the truck to take it away. We're not capable of hauling it on our backs. The Seventh Step says we don't have to.

I have prepared myself to let go of the old masks, weapons, and hiding places. I don't need them anymore.

*I want to believe, and I do believe that
someday I will.*

— *Toni J.*

Most of us have learned to have more faith in things than in relationships. We believe our tires will give us 30,000 miles, but have little faith our loved ones will provide such dependability. Too often, this is the attitude with which we approach our Higher Power.

When the program asks that we "come to believe," all the old tapes start playing: "You'd better not count on it" or "It's a nice idea, but it probably won't work for me."

But no one "comes to believe" all at once. Not fully. And the program doesn't require that. What it does require is putting one foot in front of the other and moving ever forward.

Recovery is a spiritual walk. As many of us start out, we scarcely believe that the sun will rise tomorrow. When we begin, we're full of hurt and desire — not wisdom and strength. Slowly is the only way we can go. Belief in ourselves, in our program, and in our Higher Power is not impossible, but it is rarely immediate. Instead, it grows slowly as we learn to trust.

Today, I pray for patience in the face of my own distrust.

The ever importunate murmur, "Dramatize it, dramatize it!"
— *Henry James*

Adult children may enter adulthood feeling irrevocably shattered and scarred. Some may make an entertainment, even a sideline career, out of telling and retelling all the unhappy details of the family squabbles — the intensity, the frequency, the pain of the wounds. Like all accounts that are repeated often and dramatically, our story, too, grows as it goes.

Beyond a certain point — certainly beyond healthy catharsis — we need to examine our motives for dramatizing our story. Are we boasting, blaming, or making excuses? Are we sincerely sharing our experience with newcomers who may identify and profit from it? Or are we wallowing in past miseries and binding ourselves to old resentments? Is the "today" part of our story as vividly explained as the "yesterday" part?

It's a good idea from time to time to listen to what we're saying and to be aware of why we're saying it. If telling our story doesn't serve a good purpose, there's no purpose in telling it.

I will keep a close watch on my motives.

God help the poor "baby" in a relationship with a nonrecovering caretaker.
— *Marge T.*

When we grow up learning we are "good" to the extent that we take care of other people, we go right on believing that everybody's happiness and success is up to us. We become so responsible that being responsible is all we know how to be. Often, we marry babies so we'll have plenty to be responsible for.

Many of us panic when we realize the mistake we've made. At first we may try to romanticize the trap we've fallen into. Next we may recognize the trap but feel too depressed to do anything about it. Finally though, with a little help from God and our other friends, we find the courage to think and act in new ways. As we persist, we're often amazed at how competent our "babies" can be, once we nudge them out of the nest.

Try it. It works. Almost no mistakes are fatal.

I will refuse to enable, understanding that to enable is to cripple the one I love.

August

Progress always involves risk. You can't steal second with your foot on first.

— Mary R.

Recovery is risk — because recovery is progress. It is doing something different, something new. It is going into areas where we have not been before.

Much of the risk, however, is more in our heads than in fact. If we have learned that everyone looks down on us or that no one values our opinion, it can be a terrible risk to say, "This is what I think." But chances are, no one would care but us. If we believe we don't deserve nice things, it may feel risky to shop for new furniture or new clothes — but no one knows but us. If we believe we shall never have any discretionary income, it may seem an impossible task to budget and save some money that is just ours. But when we open a savings account, no one knows but us.

Sure it is a risk to take off for second. But we'll never get home if we don't leave first base.

With the help of my Higher Power, I am willing and able to venture into unfamiliar territory.

August 2

*If you do not find peace in yourself you
will never find it anywhere else.*
— *Paula A. Bendry*

Peace is not won by contention, chance, or submission. And there is no such thing as peace by
acquisition of money or fame. No outside reality,
as a matter of fact, can make good on the promise
of peace.

Some people from dysfunctional families live in
the light of peace, and some from seemingly ideal
families have lives of constant chaos. Poor people
include both the happy and the miserable, just as
wealthy people do. Neither money nor background guarantees a peaceful heart.

Who we are right now is the central issue — not
what we possess or where we came from. Peace is
an inner reality for those who come to accept that
which cannot be changed, and take up the struggle
against that which can and must be dealt with.

Because peace is a prize of the spirit, it is accessi-
ble to all of us.

*Peace in my world begins and ends with me. If
there is unrest in my heart, I will look only to
myself and my Higher Power for a solution.*

*If we won't listen we won't hear the
music.*

— *Eric M.*

What are we? A hank of hair and a piece of
bone? A few cents' worth of minerals? Or are we
each a song? A unique chord struck deliberately to
add to the infinite harmony of the universe?

Many of us would *like* to agree with the last
definition, but we dare not. We are sure that we
are out of tune because too many of our notes are
flat. We don't listen because we're afraid of what
we might hear. We're certain we wouldn't like it.

The consequence is that we would rather do almost anything than be quiet and listen. We work
too much, run too much, talk too much — anything so we won't have to listen.

But the hymn of the universe goes on whether
we're listening or not. So we might as well tune in.
Perhaps our spirits will be smoothed enough to let
our heads entertain some new ideas like "I'm not so
bad. My note is a good sound."

With practice, we can become very good at being still and listening. And in stillness, we can understand that the hymn wouldn't be the same without our notes.

I pray for the courage to listen.

August 4

Men at some time are masters of their fates.

— *William Shakespeare*

A very common line of talk heard among adult children is how often we abdicate participation in our own lives. We tend to turn a fearful, deaf ear to the decision-making process that determines our fate.

The pattern seems to be that when conflict arises, we compulsively choose from a variety of ill-fated responses. A common one is to jump headfirst into our fear of abandonment pool at the first sight of conflict. This is a choice to close our ears and hearts so we can disengage from what is going on. From such a distanced position, of course, we have no input into resolutions and outcomes.

But that can change. We can change. A member shared just such a turnaround when she said, "My new experience is to hang in there no matter what. The appearance of conflict does not mean that I have to run. I can stay. I can listen. I can participate, and I can really feel good about both the process and the result."

God grant me the courage to face conflict without running. I am becoming more responsible every day.

Be still, and know that I am God.
— *Psalms 46:10*

How do we approach prayer? There's a world of difference, isn't there, between "Listen, Lord, your servant speaks" and "Speak, Lord, your servant listens"? Just as your child's request for an expensive toy is different from his request that you take him on your lap and sing to him. One is a bid for love and sharing; the other is more of a demand for a gift.

Receptivity is crucial to all relationships. We have to be quiet and listen if we want to set the stage for conscious contact. If we don't listen, we don't hear, and if we don't hear, we can't know who the other is and what the other is saying. Perhaps we're afraid to listen too closely to God, afraid that He will communicate disappointment and disapproval. Or perhaps we're afraid that God will remain silent.

Opening up is the only way to prove the matter. Making the connection is the only way to hear the new song.

I commit myself to regularly listen to the "word that is me."

August 6

> *I've created many a nightmare by in-
> sisting on my own way.*
>
> — *Eamon O.*

Oh, how we love to get our own way! What should happen, when it should happen, who should do what, and how they should do it — we know *exactly* how the scene should play. If only they all understood what's good for them — as we do.

We all have our moments, of course. Times when events and other people seem to bend to our will. For a moment we taste a sweet power. But the satisfaction doesn't last. Perhaps our manipulations backfire. Or perhaps later events prove that our way was the wrong way.

Realistically, forcing a river never works. The longer we practice our program, the more we learn to surrender the certainty that we "know." The fact is that none of us *knows* what should happen, let alone when and how. The fact is our best guesses are just as likely to be wrong as they are right. And the fact behind those two facts is that exciting new insights can only come to those who know that they don't know.

Today, I pray for humility. Today I will practice formulating good questions rather than bad answers.

*It is not easy to find happiness in our-
selves, and it is not possible to find it
elsewhere.*

— *Agnes Replier*

There is a curious phenomenon found among
many adult children called switching addictions. It
may not truly be addictions one is talking about
but the dynamics are similar; we become obses-
sively involved in one activity as an excuse, and an
escape, from dealing with another.

Rather than deal with many core issues such as
emotional dependency, shame, or fear of abandonment, adult children may seek freedom from
outside activities. We may become compulsive ex-
ercisers, or seek happiness by spending, eating, or
collecting romantic involvements like charms on a
bracelet.

Happiness cannot be found outside ourselves. If
the inner core of control and satisfaction is not
there, no matter what else we may surround ourselves with (or deny ourselves), we remain barren.

*I accept responsibility for my own happiness, for
the obstacles I put in my own way, and for the
happiness substitutes that I use to distract myself.*

August 8

*The healthier we become, the less will-
ing we become to tolerate disaster in
our relationships.*
— Mary Catherine North

"Are there any good men out there?" "Why can't
I find a good old-fashioned woman? Maybe they
don't make them anymore!" How often we hear
sentiments like these from lonely people who, try
as they might, always come out losers in their relationships.

But there is no accident or mystery or bad luck
involved when we consistently fail to make solid
relationships. We find partners who fit and go after them. If the people who "fit" us aren't good
possibilities, the pattern of misfit must have more
to do with us than it does with them.

But when we come to believe that we deserve to
be respected, that we do not tolerate abuse, and
that a loving relationship can be part of life —
that's when it all becomes possible.

We are as good as anybody else. We deserve
respect and happiness. When we believe these
truths, our "luck" in relationships will change.

*Today, I will not look in anybody else for what I
can only find in myself.*

*Others treat us the way we invite them
to treat us.*

— Barb H.

Coping with stress is a lot more difficult than preventing it in the first place. If we think prevention, we can avoid a surprising number of stressful situations by thinking ahead and sidestepping. We don't have to have lunch with difficult or complaining co-workers, for example. We can take a walk at lunchtime or catch up on some reading.

We can limit our availability to other family members by telling them we're off duty after 8 p.m. If we stick to it, the others will learn not to ask for late night help with homework or for a shirt to be ironed. We deserve the rest and the quiet time that builds up our reserves and fends off stress. Giving all our time away is foolish, not virtuous. We can only expect others to respect our limitations if we are clear about our boundaries.

To stay healthy, we need to avoid, or at least limit, involvement in all unnecessary aggravations.

I will demand the time I need each day for myself.

August 10

*No life is so hard that you can't make it
easier by the way you take it.*
— *Ellen Glasgow*

Friendly fire is a military term meaning attack from your own side. A man at a meeting of adult children used the term to describe what was happening in his own life. He was identifying himself as the sniper on his own position.

He said that he had equipped himself with a lethal arsenal of self-pity and resentment and had carried it around with him "just in case." Of course he found plenty of targets — as we all find plenty of opportunities to feel cheated or sorry for ourselves. So he unleashed one deadly volley after another — on himself.

Many of us are victims of self-created friendly fire. No one makes us do it; we do it ourselves. But we do have the power, as the man in the meeting did, to see what's going on and to stop it. If we refuse to pull the trigger, we may well find that our own war with life has been mostly of our making.

Today, I value serenity above all else. I no longer have a need for contention — with myself or anybody else.

*I always warned my little brother,
"Don't tell! No matter who asks, don't
tell!"*

— *Madeline C.*

Adult children are all too familiar with keeping
quiet and laying low. We knew it was our job,
though it wasn't always stated, to keep the blanket
of secrecy tucked in tight. "They" — our friends,
teachers, neighbors — must never know. So we
said nothing. Ever.

For many of us, not talking became a habit. And
so did defensiveness, rationalization, and lying. To
us, leaping from a plane without a parachute
would have felt less dangerous than talking freely
to a friend. "Sharing is dangerous!" the old tapes
cry out when we momentarily relax in comrade-
ship.

The task is to let go of the long-held secrets. No
matter how painful the opening up process may
be, it is absolutely essential to recovery. For us,
sharing means heartache and happiness, triumph
and tragedy — one the wellspring of the other.
Silence is the prison; sharing is the key.

*Today, I will remember that trusting a friend is not
dangerous and will open myself to honest sharing.*

August 12

We are healed of a suffering only by experiencing it to the full.
— *Marcel Proust*

Healing is a mysterious, complex process. In each of us, healing follows its own time line and its own course. Most often we can see healing take place in others far more easily than we can see it in ourselves. Our own healing takes us by surprise; we're oftentimes only aware of it after the fact.

A situation that would once have triggered a burst of anger somehow doesn't have the power to set us off. A painful old memory bobs up without the stomach knots that used to accompany it. A week goes by, then a month, before we realize that not one dreadful thing happened; we've had thirty good days in a row!

One day, perhaps suddenly, we realize that our lives are not the same as they were. Something has happened. We are changed. What was broken is becoming whole. Bitterness that could "never" be dislodged has shifted and diminished. And then we know miracles are possible, even for us.

I believe that the benefits of recovery are limitless. Today, I am patient, confident, and willing to be healed.

Lovers, children, heroes, none of them
do we fantasize as extravagantly as we
fantasize our parents.
— *Francine Du Plessix Gray*

Other people's parents could have all sorts of
flaws and quirks and problems. We not only didn't
mind, but we may well have found their foibles
sympathetic, interesting, or even endearing. We
didn't despise them if they lost their jobs or got
sick. We didn't expect them to be anything but
human. People are people; on some level, we accepted that.

Our own parents, on the other hand, were supposed to be straight out of a fantasy family on TV.
Our mothers, who were supposed to have been
prettier, should have made cookies for us every
afternoon. Our fathers, who were supposed to be
taller, should have been Scout leaders and PTA
presidents. Since myth is always larger than life,
their failures were also in mythical proportion.
Their mistakes were inexcusable; their sickness
was treachery.

In fact, they may not have been much different
from other people's parents — except for the roles
we assigned to them.

My own growth allows me to see other people —
including my parents — in a new light.

> *I learned how to survive, but not how to live.*
>
> — *Gilly A.*

We adult children spent much of our childhood learning how to get by. Many of us didn't learn to play as other children play or to observe and describe reality as other children do. We didn't learn to laugh at happy things and cry at sad things. We learned to coast. To fake it. To imitate as best we could the look and behavior of the people we imagined were "normal." We survived as well as we could.

Some of us made a better show of it than others. Some of us — twenty, thirty, or forty years away from the days of our childhood — have gone on to lives of outstanding professional achievement. We tell ourselves it doesn't matter now. The past is past. Others of us are never free of haunting images. To us, then is now, the sense of loss is constant, and the pain, like the sun, greets us every day. We have no energy for achievement.

Both categories of adult children are caught in the same trap. Without a desire to confront and resolve past issues, neither has escaped "what was." Both are still "getting by." There is no way out but through.

Today, I pray for strength to choose life over survival.

The lowest ebb is the turn of the tide.
— Henry Wadsworth Longfellow

Sometimes our relationships have to get worse before they can get better. Sometimes, in fact, pain in a relationship may mean that we're doing something *right* — perhaps for the first time.

Many adult children grow up with some abnormal habits and patterns that, over time, come to feel "normal." Often, we don't become aware that these patterns are unhealthy until we are recovering. And by then these behaviors are thoroughly woven into our adult relationships. When we begin to change them, we also change the original ground rules of the relationship. As we start to think and act differently, we throw our partners off just as surely as if we started to tango in the middle of a waltz.

Some relationships don't survive the changes. But many are saved because the recovering person had the courage to change the music and persist in the new steps until equilibrium could be regained.

I have confidence in the new direction I am taking. In the long run I trust that all will be well for me and mine.

> *I haven't won yet but I haven't lost,*
> *either.*
>
> — *Dennis C.*

A favorite saying in sports is, "It isn't losing to get knocked down. Losing is staying down."

In life as in sports, that idea makes great sense. Like "Let go and let God," or "Let it begin with me," it is a saying that reminds us of an important underlying principle. In this case the principle is that battles aren't wars, but rather a series of campaigns. No one wins every time out, or can expect to. And some battles aren't worth fighting anyway.

Fighting a battle isn't hell — our unrealistic expectations are. When we strike out against some old attitude or behavior, we have to realize we're in for the long haul. When the enemy is some aspect of ourselves, we are up against a formidable opponent that won't give up easily. We have to expect that there will be many battles — and not a few defeats. The winner is the one who perseveres longest.

Only continued effort wins the war; we can't lose if we don't quit.

Today, I pray for persistence in the face of many defeats. I ask my Higher Power for courage to keep at it.

*If you want to be found, stand where
the seeker seeks.*

— Sidney Lanier

When does a good program turn into a bad program? When it becomes a hiding place. As adult children, we are good — no, ingenious — at finding hiding places.

Sometimes we hide behind our work by staying super busy. We hide in prayer itself — behind sweet-sounding words. We can choose to always be tired so we can hide in sleep. We can hide behind any of the "helper" roles by fixing others so we never have to fix ourselves. We can hide behind self-effacement by telling others how "hopeless" we are, so no one will expect us to get better. We can even make our program a hiding place by going through the motions, saying all the right things, but never really encountering ourselves.

If we want to be found, we have to come out where somebody can find us.

I will identify my hiding places and make conscious decisions about choosing them or not.

August 18

Admitting error clears the score
And proves you wiser than before.
*   — Arthur Guiterman*

Much of the chaos in our lives can be directly traced to our own lopsided values. Not only do we act out these beliefs more than we think we do, we may be fiercely loyal to the very belief systems that fill our lives with hurt and pain.

Unaware, we may be completely devoted to perfectionism, martyrdom, rigidity, or the belief that life is supposed to be miserable. If we think of it at all, we probably call these traits other names, like idealism, generosity, firmness, and realism. But by any name, these beliefs invariably generate corresponding behavior, which in turn manufactures chaos as efficiently as if it were being cranked out on a conveyor belt.

When chaos appears in our lives, it is beneficial to look for the underlying belief or negative value that created the behavior that created the chaos. Sometimes it's not the behavior that needs to be changed — it's the long-held idea hiding behind it.

Today, I have the courage to reevaluate old assumptions.

I asked God to be present in my life.
And that presence was there.
— Johnny C.

Prayers are an essential element of a spiritual life. But the prayers themselves are not the spiritual life — they are manifestations of it. Just as diamonds are not the diamond mine, but the expression of its wealth, prayers are expressions of the richness within.

A spiritual life is always open to the spirit, alert and responsive to the Higher Power's will as it is expressed in daily communication. Of course there cannot be any communication without conscious contact.

Words are the wings of love. If we don't verbalize what we think and feel, neither the others nor ourselves can come to a deeper understanding, a closer sharing.

The words we speak to our Higher Power need not be formal or ritualistic. The form of the prayer is much less important than the motivation for the prayer. The reaching out and speaking out is the prayer.

Today, I will initiate conscious contact with my Higher Power. I will see this not as an obligation but as an invitation to love.

August 20

Death is the mother of beauty.
— *Wallace Stevens*

Death, like birth, is natural. Our feelings about it aside, death is not a mistake that can be avoided or an outrage that should be protested. Death is a part of life — it is the last stage of living. By completing the process that began at birth, a person's death makes his life whole.

Our grief at the death of a loved one is also normal and natural. And dealing with the sadness of our loss is also a process — a process that, over time, is ended and made whole. Grief is extremely personal; no two people grieve in the same way and for the same length of time. Different people's reactions can never be accurately judged or compared.

No matter what our beliefs about an afterlife, there are two unromantic but practical truths that can help anchor us when we are bereaved. One is that the person who is dead has no problems — our problem is our own sense of loss. And the second is that acceptance of death, like acceptance of our past, is the way of the wise.

I rejoice that my loved one and I had some time together. I am grateful as well as grief-stricken.

We don't have time not to have time.
— *Gary Burke*

To develop the habit of reflection means to take the time, regularly and often, to listen to ourselves, to ask how things are going, to think about what things we did today that were successful, and what things we did that were not so successful. When we reflect, we bend back to see where we have been so we can know where to go next.

Reflection breeds insight. "I never thought of it that way," can become a way of life, a limitless opportunity. *But we must stand in the way of it* if we want to see life and its possibilities in a new way. We have to make the time to reflect, and we have to stick with it until the thoughts flow. At times our minds have to be literally pried open to make room for the fresh air of new ideas: reflection is the tool to use.

I will daily examine my life to see if I have taken the time to walk my road of recovery.

August 22

> *The smartest thing I ever said was, "Help me!"*
>
> — *Dorrie T.*

How difficult it is to acknowledge that we need help! How it goes against the grain to admit we are needy. But "Help me!" is the password that opens the door to recovery.

When we say these words to our Higher Power, spouse, or friend, we are really saying we are ready to be honest. For some of us, this may be the first honest personal statement we have made in many years.

When we ask others to help us learn to be free, to deal with our illusions, to shuck off our compulsions, we are asking them to help us turn on the light. Only the light of honesty can show us our hidden immaturities and stumbling-block character defects. Childish temper tantrums disguised as righteous indignation must be seen for what they are. The inability to accept love must not be allowed to wear the mask of sophistication. Are we too cool to be caught or too scared to be honest?

Some things are just too difficult to figure out without a little help from our friends.

Today, I will come closer to freedom by asking someone who is honest to help me be honest.

*The ability to accept responsibility is
the measure of the man.*
— *Roy L. Smith*

When something new comes to be, we can be sure there was courage in the background, propelling it forward. As the quality of heart and head that resists and challenges the status quo, courage is the fuel of possibility.

Recovery is creation of new realities. If fear and panic dominated our old attitude toward life, then courage — even if it is a tiny spark — is what enables us to act as if we are confident until we, in fact, become confident. If a sense of alienation and aloneness was our reality, it is courage that tugs us out of the corner and into the group, courage that opens our mouths to speak, and courage that keeps us there until fellowship becomes more real than alienation ever was.

Courage is a key. It opens the door to kindness, wisdom, and honesty. But unless we use that key, we'll never get to the other side of the door.

Today, I will move boldly toward my goals even though I do not feel a bit bold. Fear will not hold me back today.

> *Good people are good because they've*
> *come to wisdom through failure.*
> — *William Saroyan*

Many of us grew up with the injunctions — do it faster, do it better, do more. Instant, complete success was the only success. Since this is impossible, we experienced only failure and expected only more failure, despite success.

Nothing can be learned — from playing the flute to hitting home runs — without failing along the way. We cannot grow if we never fail. Attitude is the difference between those who fail and see it as an opportunity to learn and those who fail and see it as another proof of their incompetence.

As we embrace the journey of recovery we will fail, we will slip, we will periodically revert to old patterns and old behaviors — that does not brand us as failures. It offers us a chance, rather, to learn more about ourselves and how better to plot strategies to avoid or to rise above the slippery spots in the future.

I don't have to hide my failures anymore — not from myself or anyone else. I am learning to make stepping-stones of my mistakes.

*The love of God is passionate. He pur-
sues each of us even when we know it
not.*

— *William Wordsworth*

A woman at a meeting of adult children recently
told of a deal she had made with God. She promised God she would stop smoking if God would
help her son get off drugs. A lively discussion en-
sued. Most were of the belief that God doesn't
bargain — not because God isn't sympathetic —
but because He has already given that which we
try to bargain for.

Isn't that a wondrous truth? God already loves
our loved ones even more than we do. And because God loves them, they have already been
gifted with everything they need. Why do we
imagine that we need to manipulate God? God is
doing everything, short of interfering with our free
will, to assist us and our loved ones along the road
to recovery and freedom.

As long as it may take and as hard as it may be,
we need to accept the incredible fact that the prize
is already won, and all we need to do is open up
and receive it.

*Today, I weigh the love I feel for my family, and I
am comforted to know they are loved even more
by God.*

> *Pain is short, and joy is eternal.*
> — *Johann Schiller*

Pain can be a teacher. And like many other teachers, pain deserves a better, more attentive audience than it sometimes gets. We can become so used to pain that we ignore it. Worse yet, our pain may be so commonplace we don't even recognize it as pain.

Many of us shame-based people don't know that everyone doesn't have pain all the time. We simply don't know that pain and living are not synonymous — or that abuse is not normal.

But pain carries a message. Pain is telling us that something is wrong, that we need to behave differently, that what hurts must be fixed. It isn't normal to feel lonely, fearful, enraged, or lost all the time. If that's the way it is for us, then we need to talk to a friend, to read, and to meditate — to do whatever it takes to pry open the doors of our minds until we understand that pain should not be the norm. Pain need not be the norm. And with the help of our Higher Power and our fellow pilgrims, pain shall not be the norm!

I am willing to reach out for help when I need it. I no longer accept hopelessness as a way of life.

Where does all the fake love come from? Is it them or is it me?

— Mel K.

The more precious any treasure is, the more fakes are created around it. And what is a greater treasure than love?

Inauthentic love abounds, and every variety is hollow at its core. Some of it is just plain deception: If you love me, you will lie for me, cheat for me, look the other way, let me do whatever I want. Some fakes are more subtle: If you love me, you will flatter me, laugh at all my jokes, buy me expensive presents, never hurt my feelings.

Real loving is so difficult that the substitutes may seem more attractive. Authentic love is trusting; fake love is not. Authentic love dares to try. How many times we think of saying, doing, or writing something to express our love! But most of the time we don't do it because we're afraid of the consequences. They might think we are foolish; they might not understand. In short, we don't trust. But their ability to understand and trust isn't the problem — ours is.

Today, I will search my heart for phony ideas about love. I will begin preparing myself to give the gift of trust.

Blessed are those who can give without remembering and take without forgetting.

— *Melvin Schleeds*

To be human is to be both a giver and a taker. Everyone alive engages in both. We give into the world order, the fruit of our daily work and effort, the grace of our being. Every smile, every word of comfort, every resisted temptation, and every bead of sweat over our work are valid contributions, no matter how minute, to the quality of human life. Every time we eat food grown by another, wear clothes that someone else sewed, or attend a meeting that someone else organized, we take.

The central issue of giving and taking is not *if*, but *how*. What is our attitude? Do we see our giving as doing our part, nothing more or less? Are we grateful for what we take? When we recognize that our life is part of a greater whole, we escape the loneliness of isolation and find new meaning in the word *sharing*.

Today, I celebrate the fact that I have an integral place in the human order. I am not "other than"; I am just as necessary as everybody else.

*Made a list of all persons we had
harmed, and became willing to make
amends to them all.*

— *Step Eight of*
Alcoholics Anonymous

In our quest for physical, mental, and spiritual health, we realize that resentments cause spiritual heart attacks. A heart that carries a lot of resentment is a heart at risk.

Step Eight provides a remedy for resentments. It tells us to get ready to make amends. It says we begin by first becoming willing to admit the wrong we have done to others.

When we make a list of such people, when we review the names and the reasons we've written these names down, we are looking at the very path to our liberation. The guilt and shame that are always attached to resentments have been a burden for too long. They've weighted down our hearts and crushed our self-esteem.

We have unfinished business with the people on that list. But for now, in Step Eight, we do nothing but work at becoming willing to reach out with our amends.

I am learning to recognize my own contribution to my heartaches. I am willing to square accounts with people I have wronged.

August 30

> *Life is not a problem to be solved but a*
> *reality to be experienced.*
> — *Soren Kierkegaard*

Problems are often teachers. As we continue to recover, we come to value the lessons learned through our problems. But "problem thinking" can be a problem in itself, strangely enough. It can become an addiction and an escape from life.

What happens if our most rewarding communication comes from sharing our problems with friends? What if our deepest sense of inner strength is only felt when we're wrestling with a difficulty? What if we get to feel so comfortable in the midst of problems that we stir up a few if we start to run out? (Don't laugh. Many of us do exactly that.)

Creating a struggle around every circumstance may give us a sense of accomplishment — but it surely makes life harder than it needs to be. The high of engaging in battle is not the only high there is. We can make connections and get good feelings in more direct and joyful ways.

I will not define my life by my problems. I remind myself that struggle is part of life — not life itself.

*Apologizing with words isn't the same
thing as apologizing with actions.*
— *Laura J.*

The old Chinese saying "Talk doesn't cook rice"
emphasizes an important principle in successful
human relations. The point is that saying and doing are different things. People can say they're
sorry every day or ten times a day. But the proof of
that sorrow is what they are doing to break the
cycle that caused the pain in the first place.

Certainly we are striving to become understanding people. It's admirable and healing to do what
we can to understand the other person.

But understanding must not be used as an excuse for unacceptable behavior. It may be that the
communication actually called for is this: "Stop
telling me you're sorry and start fixing what's broken. Don't tell me; show me!" No human being
can have too much understanding. But we have to
remember that understanding without accountability is just excuse making.

*Today, I will examine my relationships for mutual
accountability. I will look closely for patterns of
apology that aren't followed up with action.*

September

*Oh Lord, thou givest us everything, at
the price of an effort.*
                    — *Leonardo da Vinci*

Balance is necessary in every area of life. Understanding the role God plays in our lives is no different. One perception is that we need do nothing, that God will do it for us. All we need to do is ask, sit back, and wait for the miracles to happen.

The other extreme approaches reality as if it really doesn't matter whether God exists or not. Anything that happens, some of us reason, will be the fruit of our own work if it's going to happen at all. So we forge ahead on our own power, assuming it will see us through.

In the middle is the balanced view that God is indeed a willing, generous giver who has already placed many gifts on our doorstep. Our job is to do the work that will enable us to open the door. It's hard to imagine anyone more gifted than the brilliant da Vinci. God gave him great talent. But we also have to remember that da Vinci often worked eighteen-hour days.

I accept the fact that I have a lot of footwork to do. I will do my part and trust in God to do His.

September 2

Every mountain and hill shall be made low; and the crooked shall be made straight, and the rough places plain.
— Isaiah 40:4

Recovery can be compared to climbing a hill. And as with all skills, the more we practice the better we become. There comes a time in the course of recovery when we view a hill that once would have caused us to quake in our boots or to quit all together. But using the skills achieved by working an intelligent, consistent program we can simply take it in stride.

When we came into the program, we were asked if we were willing to go to any lengths to win our freedom from bondage. As we grew and developed a positive response, all sorts of things became possible that at one time were not. We are often told in the program that "the best way to eat an elephant is one bite at a time." We don't have to do it all at once. All recovery is made inch by inch.

Now we can look at yonder hill and accept it as just another obstacle to be conquered — and not a very big obstacle at that.

I am amazed and encouraged by the gains I've already made. Today's challenges do not intimidate me.

Less is more.

— Robert Browning

Adult children are often compulsive. Why? Are we now, perhaps decades later, still chasing the acceptance and approval we were never given? Do we find ourselves running this way and that, attempting impossible tasks, accepting unrealistic burdens? Why? Are we trying to reach back through the mist of the past to court what was never there? Isn't the prize we seek only found in the present?

We need to slow down enough to think before we act. Before we say yes, we need to look at what is being asked. We need to determine if it's what we want to do, if it's good for us to do, and whether we have time. Just because something needs doing doesn't mean we have to do it or that it won't get done without us.

Much of our busy-ness doesn't make sense. Often we need to do less, not more.

I can simplify my life and lighten my burdens by deciding realistically what I want to do and what I have time to do.

September 4

They believed they could, and they could. I believe I can too.

— Lou O.

Sometimes it feels like working on ourselves is challenge enough — working on our relationships is maybe more than we can manage. We get discouraged when we realize that the skills that make relationships work are the skills we never learned — skills like trusting, identifying our needs and feelings, asking for what we need, saying how we feel, and recognizing the boundaries between ourselves and others. The things we're not very good at make quite a list. We can look at that list, then at ourselves, then at our partners, and think we don't have a chance.

Then we think again. We remember the skills we have learned since we came into the program. We remember some of the recovery stories we've heard in meetings. Wonderful, exciting stories from people who could never express themselves — but learned to do so; people who would not know intimacy if it came up and bit them — but who now could write a book on the subject. Skills are learned. Learning takes time. Hang in there.

Today, I pray for patience with my limitations and faith in the limitless benefits of the program as it works in my life.

For as he thinks within himself, so he is.

— Proverbs 23:7

What we think about, we talk about. And what we talk about, we bring about. Sooner or later, the thoughts that forecasted reality become reality, at least as far as we are able to know. Suppose that each of us had a recorder taping our thoughts, rather than our words, for a whole day. What would we hear when we played the tape? Would our thoughts be mostly focused on the injustices of life and the slim chances we have of ever making progress? Or would our thoughts be positive, appreciative, and hopeful about ourselves and our world?

Good thoughts bring good things. When we think in terms of the goodness of life, we see the good, talk the good, and the good will come to be part of our lives.

I will examine each day the quality of my thoughts.

September 6

They love the best who love with compassion.

— *Ellen Anne Hill*

Lucky indeed is the person who is loved by those with compassion. Hard indeed is the lot of those loved by rigid boundaries, quick judgments, and a small sense of humanity.

All of us are fighting a personal battle, all of us have been scarred, and all of us are riddled with contradictions and inconsistent behavior. To be human is to be flawed. Compassion is the state of being in touch with the bright, beautiful, and flawed nature of humanity.

Compassionate people are able to see the gold beneath the metal. They are able to see the effort beneath the occasional failure. They are able to see the intention beneath the mistake.

We have all made mistakes, experienced pain, and learned to heal. Where would we be — when the wounds are fresh — without the compassion of others?

I am aware that life is difficult for everyone. Today, I will be especially sensitive and kind.

'Tis only God may be had for the asking.
>   — *James Russell Lowell*

"There's no such thing as a free lunch" is certainly true of most things. If we want flowers, we have to dig. If we yearn for the prize, we have to win it. We get nothing that we don't earn and pay for — except the one thing which is most important — God's friendship and love.

God alone, as each of us understands Him to be, comes freely to anyone with an open heart. The least socially acceptable person in this world is acceptable to God. The divine gift is always there for the asking.

Why do we wear ourselves out rushing after meaningless trinkets and pats on the head when all the while, just outside the door of decision, is the power and the love that make all things possible and precious?

I will determine what is important in each day and what is not — and let that guide my decisions.

September 8

We cannot do everything at once, but
we can do something at once.
— Calvin Coolidge

Big leaps are often made over time — one small
step after another. The smallest action, taken in
favor of recovery, may be just the impetus needed
for yet another small step, and then another until
we've made a quantum jump forward.

Many of us balk at the slow and steady strategy.
We want the big win now, all at once. We don't
want to work to *get* there — we want to *be* there.
For many of us, this need to have it all and to have
it all at once has been a problem for us for much of
our lives. Now we have the opportunity to work a
program that emphasizes steadiness, perseverence,
and patience. When we see our impatience as an
obstacle to our recovery, we are better able to rejoice in each baby step we take. Our impatient
natures have longed for instant recovery, but our
recovery program encourages a calmer, more even,
approach toward ourselves. Let's move on now —
steadily, surely, with no concern of how slowly —
before we stop taking the small steps that big leaps
are made of.

Today, I will check and see if I have been patient
with myself and the lovely, new world I am build-
ing.

Yesterday's answer has nothing to do with today's problem.

— *Stu B.*

As little kids, many of us learned to disconnect from pain rather than stay attached. We separated ourselves from the action around us in order to survive. Over time, what we did is what we became — separate. Having almost literally burned the bridge between us and others, we see now that we are stranded. The isolation that was meant to keep anyone from getting at us also keeps anyone from getting to us.

We need to rebuild the bridge. People, like islands, need ways to see and reach and touch hands over all that separating water. Making connections is the only way. Unless we can hear each other singing and crying, unless we can comfort each other's failures and cheer each other's victories, we are missing out on the best that life has to offer. The only real action takes place on the bridge between people.

Today, I ask my Higher Power for the courage to build another bridge.

September 10

*The man who makes no mistakes does
not usually make anything.*
　　　　　— Edward Phelps

At times, our fear of making mistakes leads us
to do nothing. Some adult children are so afraid of
the censure and degradation they experienced in
the past they will procrastinate forever to avoid a
risk.

But calculated risk is what it takes to make improvement in our lives. We can learn to see the
possibility of gain as well as the possibility of failure when we come up against a chance-taking situation. If we can see both, we can make a clearer,
less fearful decision about what to do.

Slowly, as we continue our road of recovery, we
may come to understand risk, not as an invitation
to disaster, but as an opportunity for growth
Growth not just in the sense of business or mone-
tary gain, but growth in the sense of discovering
new adventures. When we grow in our ability to
enjoy life we discover excitement, and the thrill of
learning that we indeed are capable of coping with
and conquering new situations.

*I will be aware of all the possible new adventures
awaiting me if only I am willing to take an intelligent risk.*

The hand that holds the whip over our heads is most often our own.
— *Harvey Eagan*

We must learn to be as patient with ourselves as God is with us. That's a tall order for adult children who, almost by definition, can't tolerate imperfection in themselves. Instead of having to "Be perfect and be perfect now," most of us need to be far less critical of ourselves. We need to give ourselves a break.

When we forgive ourselves for being human we are acting as God acts toward us. God knows who and what we are. He doesn't expect perfection. We're the ones who do that.

Playing both taskmaster and whipping boy at the same time is too much for anybody. It is an example of a classic double bind that plagues so many adult children.

We need to learn to be neither tyrant nor cringing victim. The task is to learn to establish sane boundaries and learn that, because we are special and deserving of marvelous things, we don't have to abuse ourselves by unrealistic expectations, or minimize our successes.

Today, I will examine my expectations and celebrate my successes.

September 12

An error, gracefully acknowledged, is a victory won.
— *Caroline Gascoigne*

Not only is it human to err, it is inevitable. There are no perfect people — but there are people who learn from their mistakes. For the most part we grow because of our mistakes, not in spite of them.

We adult children tend to hide our mistakes behind delusion and denial. Rather than identify with this most human of all traits, we have a lot of trouble permitting ourselves to be just as flawed as everyone else. Why? Because we're still trying to protect ourselves from dangerous situations — situations that, most of the time, no longer exist.

For us especially, graceful acknowledgment of an error is a victory of the highest order. Not only is it the adult, reasonable thing to do — it is another giant step away from the demeaning bonds of the past.

I will admit my mistakes when they occur and endeavor to find what lesson they contain.

I asked God for new eyes and ears.
— *Eleanor K.*

We can give millions to charity and have no charity. We can read all the poetry in the library and not be able to appreciate a single poetic thought. We can look at every great painting in the world and find no beauty.

If there is emotional and spiritual poverty in our lives, the problem isn't *out there*, it's *in here.* Blaming early disadvantage is no good. Many advantaged people are in the same boat as we are. And many joyful souls, burdened by horrendous disadvantages we'd never swap for, find beauty and delight everywhere they look.

What's the difference? The world they live in is the same as ours, yet their involvement in it is different. They stopped hoping to hear a good song and started singing one. They are in touch with their own specialness, which in turn connects with the specialness all around them. We already have everything we need to be joyful. The quality of what passes between the world and ourselves is a matter of personal growth.

Today, I ask my Higher Power for a surer sense of my own specialness.

September 14

The condition upon which God has given liberty to man is eternal vigilance.

— *John Philpot Curran*

Stinking thinking is as durable as crabgrass. It pops right back almost as soon as we can root it out. So we shouldn't be surprised — even if we're working the program to the best of our ability — to find thoughts of self-pity, resentment, envy, and hatred showing up again and again. Such feelings and attitudes won't go away willingly. Like real weeds, these old thinking patterns are alive and deeply-rooted.

Keeping them down takes stubbornness also. Willingness to keep at it is the key. Instant control is not possible, nor is final and absolute eradication. Because we are human, our thoughts will always be somewhat wayward and disorganized; our feelings will be excessive at some moments and inappropriate at others. Perfection isn't one of our choices — no matter how hard we try.

But control is. Magnificent gardens aren't beautiful only because the flowers are so pretty — they're beautiful because someone's controlling the weeds.

I won't be discouraged by the persistence of my old ideas. I'm willing to take care of business on a daily basis.

*If one advances confidently in the di-
rection of his dreams, and endeavors to
live the life which he has imagined, he
will meet with a success unimagined in
common hours.*
— *Henry David Thoreau*

We can only do so much at any given time. And
that is enough. As events ebb and flow in our
lives, we may sometimes find ourselves in terrible
situations ranging from toxic relationships to financial chaos. How we react depends upon how
we were acting before the problem became critical.
Had we been doing our footwork? Had we built
up enough strength, one day at a time, to handle
the situation?

Before recovery, we often saw crises as beyond
our control. We tended to retreat into feelings of
self-pity and abandonment. Now we know that
there is hope and help in the form of people to talk
to, principles to apply, and tiny baby steps to take
all the way through the dark tunnel until we reach
light again. We know we can make it because
we've been pumping iron, mentally and emotionally, in the daily practice of our program.

*I will do the little things that count, creating a
massive reserve of strength against the day when
such strength is needed.*

September 16

The cause is hidden, but the result is known.

— *Ovid*

Causes bring about effects. In human behavior, we tend to get what we do. If what we do is shout a lot and shake our fists, what we get is a shortage of people who want to be around us. If what we do is withdraw and hide, what we get is loneliness and an ever-deepening sense that we are not likeable.

If what we do is get involved with people who are too selfish or crippled to hold up their end of a loving relationship, what we get is a broken heart — perhaps over and over again. On the other hand, if what we do is concentrate on making ourselves healthier and more generous people, what we get is genuine readiness for a relationship that can work. And if what we do is consistently work our program, what we get is joyous recovery.

Instead of complaining about the effects of our behavior, we could better spend our time by looking at the behavior itself. We do have choices.

Today, I won't look for apples on the lemon tree. If I want apples, I'll have to buy a different tree.

Aim for fairness!

— Dorothy L.

It has been said that we usually, eventually, hit what we aim at. That's why the popular wisdom is to aim high if you mean to be successful, keep your eye on the target, and so on.

From time to time, it is useful to ask ourselves where we are aiming our thoughts and energies. While our talk may be lofty, our walk often reveals something a good bit closer to earth.

The bottom line for many of us is the lingering sense of resentment that what happened to us wasn't fair. And of course it wasn't. The truth is that we deserved better, but the fact is that we didn't get it. So what happens to all that resentment? It grinds away in the form of preoccupation, reliving old events, and fantasizing different outcomes.

Yesterday we got what they gave us. Today we get what we give ourselves. If we eventually hit what we aim at, we could do a lot worse than aim for fairness for ourselves and others.

Today, I will be on the lookout for injustices in my personal world. I will do what I can to contribute to fairness.

September 18

Never throw mud. You may miss your
mark. And you will certainly have
dirty hands.

— *Joseph Parker*

Many are the ways to throw mud. We do just
that when we fling resentment and hatred into our
past, smear delusion and denial on our present, or
hurl negativity and self-pity into our future.

Of course we have the right to do that if we want
to. We can wallow in dirt until it becomes so normal that we don't know the difference. Usually,
nobody knows what we're up to, and we ourselves
are convinced that such behavior is only realistic.

But we're the ones who have to live with the
dirty hands. Our mud doesn't bother the people
we resent; they may not even be alive. The people
we live with now have even less to do with it. If we
look for mud, we will find it. And it will be ours
alone.

I refuse to damage myself by harboring negative
thoughts and desires.

When I want to understand what is
happening today or try to decide what
will happen tomorrow, I look back.
— *Oliver Wendell Holmes*

Some of us adult children have to divorce our
parents before we can hope to develop a healthy
marital relationship. The danger is that the new
home and family we set out to create may turn out
to be not new at all, but an extension of the home
and family we grew up in.

Until we make significant changes, our married
lives mirror the lives we know best — those of our
parents and of ourselves in relation to our parents.
We oftentimes choose mates that fit those familiar
interactions. Because all we know are the old
ways, we automatically continue to operate as we
learned to operate. And, almost as automatically,
we get disappointed enough to throw in the towel.
But divorcing our mates may not solve anything.
Maybe it's our parents we need to divorce, and the
behavior patterns we learned in their homes.
Maybe we need to develop an entirely different
way of thinking about what it takes to make relationships work.

I will create a better future by being responsible
today.

Think not because no man sees,
Such things will remain unseen.
  — Henry Wadsworth Longfellow

The visit we made although we were busy, the gift for another that cost us our lunch money, the extra lap run, the meeting we were too tired to attend — but attended anyway — they all add up. Every little thing we do has consequences. At times those consequences may seem as insignificant as the acts that caused them. Yet each one is an important contribution to who we are and who we are becoming.

The smallest acts either enrich or diminish our character. And who we are shows. No matter how quietly or privately an act is done, it is immediately transformed into the "us" that is seen by the whole world.

A brave act done in public was first accomplished in the private realm of a person's heart. A kind word said was first a kind thought. And a movement toward recovery was first willed in that part of our being that no one else ever sees.

I know that enough baby steps add up to a leap. Slow and steady is good enough for me.

Often happiness calls but we are too busy to answer.

— *Ellen H.*

In the pursuit of happiness many people are too busy to find that which they seek. Frequently the happiness we so passionately desire is found in little events that are but whispered. If we don't pay attention, we miss them.

There can be happiness in the way light falls through the trees or in the way autumn leaves flutter to the ground. There can be happiness in the way our children call for us by name or in the familiar sight of our home as we round the corner two blocks away. Happiness weaves its way through precious memories and valueless keepsakes that are priceless to us. Many take enormous delight in the presence of a beloved pet, just the way they look at us or the unconditional love they pour out upon us. For some, there is genuine delight in the taste of a specially loved food.

We are surrounded by that which can be meaningful and full of delight. The question is, will we be still and quiet long enough to enjoy?

Recovery unveils many beauties that were hidden from me before. I am amazed at the loveliness that surrounds me.

September 22

*The trouble with loving our neighbor
as ourselves is that most of us do.*
— *Toni W.*

Many people find it difficult to care about others
as much as they care about themselves. The problem for us is quite different.

We can only give what we have. And the only
love we have to give is the love that we've experienced for ourselves. That is our problem. Many of
us have learned to feel shame at every turn, to
expect abandonment, to look at the world through
dark glasses. We haven't experienced ourselves as
worthy objects of love — not often enough and
not long enough. So the love we accord to ourselves is often tentative, conditional, halfhearted,
and downright skimpy. Many of us are only able
to love ourselves as long as it doesn't inconvenience
or cause pain to others.

If we want to have more to give to others, we
must first give more to ourselves.

*Today, I will think about all the reasons I am lov-
able. I will demonstrate this love in all my deal-
ings.*

Comparisons are odious.
— *John Fortesque*

Today, we are just who we are — no more, no less. That's not a bad place to be. It's not a depressing thing to realize or an unbearable thing to accept. All the comparing we used to do was really much more painful: Do they dress better, own a bigger house, make more money? Do their spouses remember their birthdays? Do their kids get better grades? Do they have more friends?

We never won at the comparing game. We always put ourselves down for not having enough or being enough — whether we knew the facts about the others or not. We assumed, by comparing their outsides with our insides, that they were doing better. Before we started to recover, we were absolutely unable to give ourselves a break.

Isn't it a relief to let that go? Doesn't it feel good to accept ourselves as we are — not as we're afraid we are and not as we wish we were? Isn't it great to watch the world twirl — and not have to go along for the ride?

Today, I withdraw from the competition. I enjoy my life and the directions I've chosen.

September 24

*Come, my friends, 'Tis not too late to
seek a newer world.*
— *Alfred, Lord Tennyson*

We've probably all heard "too late" stories at our meetings. One such story concerns a middle-aged woman's dilemma over whether or not to go back to school. Too little money and too many family responsibilities had prevented her from becoming a nurse. "It would take me five years to finish," the woman said dejectedly, "and in five years I'll be fifty-one years old!" Whereupon her friend answered, "Okay, suppose that you don't become a nurse. *Then* how old will you be in five years?"

The point is an important one for those of us who are beginning the recovery process somewhat late in life. Rather than bewailing lost time, we need to concentrate on possibilities rather than liabilities.

It is tremendously exciting to let our minds fly toward "what if." What if I decided to learn to sail a boat, climb a mountain, become a gourmet cook? Slowly, if we don't give up, many of those what-if's become why-not's. Then we are on our way. Why not, when life is so short and we are such grand people? Why not, indeed?

Today, I will face the not yet and ask, "Why not?"

Envy's a coal comes hissing hot from hell.

— *Philip James Bailey*

A co-worker wins a grand prize in a drawing. A neighbor inherits enough money to add a room to her house and to take a great vacation. A friend's son or daughter wins a scholarship. What's our reaction? Do we automatically rejoice at someone else's good fortune? Or do we immediately sink into a pit of self-pity and resentment, having to force a smile and a word of congratulations?

Occasional flickers of envy are human and inevitable, but a chronic sense of being cheated is a sign of spiritual disorder, a sign that there's work to be done. Acceptance and gratitude are the antidotes to the misery machine of envy.

"Why not me?" in the face of another's windfall may just as logically be asked in the face of another's tragedy. Let us have the wisdom to accept our lives as they are and to be less blind to the advantages we already have.

Today, I am grateful for what I have and gracious about what other people have.

September 26

I formed my habits, and my habits formed my future.

— J. T.

Practice makes perfect.

Whether it's playing the piano or making mountains out of molehills, if we practice it long enough, we get good at it. That's what habits are — proficiencies born of practice. Habits may be conscious or unconscious, healthy or unhealthy, attractive or repulsive, important or trivial.

Our habits form our future. Just as a train is directed by the rails it rolls on, our lives are directed by our habits. Unless we build new rails, or habits, our lives will continue to move toward the same old places on the same old rails. How could it be any other way?

Habits are powerful — mostly because they're too deep to be visible. But they're there and operating all the time. We need to be aware of what our habits are. Every confrontation with an unfriendly habit is a singular victory. Every time we lay a new foot of track in a different direction we affect the quality of our future. Every time counts.

Today, I will begin making a list of my habits, both positive and negative. I will be more aware of future consequences.

Not to decide is to decide.
— *Harvey Cox*

No one can force us to make a decision we don't want to make. Until we're ready we can't force good decisions — let alone make them stick. Except for a few rare occasions we can usually get along very well without making any decisions at all. But sooner or later, decision-making time does catch up with us: We've gotten all the advice we need, thought about it, and prayed about it. The time has come.

Rather than freeze and put it off, we should remember that we only have a limited amount of time. And the quality of those days and years is totally dependent on the decisions we make. Never again will we have this hour to live over.

When the time comes, we mustn't be afraid to make any decision in favor of life. The opportunity to decide about right now will not come again. We can either look at this truth and cringe or see it as an opportunity and seize it with gratitude. It is exciting to consider that we can make decisions now, about our lives now, that will enhance our lives forever.

I will train myself when facing decisions to see them as opportunities rather than dreadful problems.

> *Made direct amends to such people*
> *wherever possible, except when to do*
> *so would injure them or others.*
> — *Step Nine of* Alcoholics Anonymous

Step Eight was the planning phase of the action we are called to take in Step Nine. Having prepared ourselves by making a list of all the persons we have harmed, we are now ready to mobilize. It's time to make contact, to acknowledge what we've done, and to say we're sorry. The purpose is not to grovel, but to take greater responsibility for our own lives.

Many adult children have found freedom at the moment they surrendered guilt by admitting wrong. Whether the admission was well received or not, whether the response of the other was appropriate or not, the sheer willingness to face up to reality was enough to unlock the shackles of the past.

When direct amends are impossible, the wisdom of the program tells us to make amends in our own hearts. Again, the upshot of Step Nine has much less to do with others than it does with our own willingness to do what it takes to recover.

My Higher Power gives me the courage to acknowledge my responsibility for hurting others.

*The winners in the program — how did
they get to be the way they are?*
— *Ivy B.*

Within the program we come across some truly
spectacular people — amazing people whose
words seem to spring from a deep well of peace.
Though their words are usually simple, their message is eloquent testimony to the profound difference between what their lives used to be and what
they are now.

As care-worn beginners on the path, we puzzle
at their progress. Sure, most of them have practiced the program longer than we have. And obviously they've found something important, something we haven't yet found.

What isn't so obvious at first is that they've also
lost something we haven't yet lost. They've let go
of some illusion, some arrogance, some imperti-
nence which we still cling to as legitimately ours,
but which only sentences us to more time on the
treadmill.

The words of those who have truly let go come
forth as a blessing: Keep going. More will be revealed.

*Today, I thank God for the presence of my brothers
and sisters in the fellowship who "keep coming
back."*

September 30

*Let not thy Will roar, when thy Power
can but whisper.*

— *Thomas Fuller*

A man at a meeting of adult children brought knowing nods and sympathetic smiles when he said, "I've found that my way doesn't always work — in fact it doesn't work very often." He was talking about the rebellious attitude he had recently discovered in himself.

Certainly, there were many in the room who could identify. The automatic "You can't make me" reaction goes back a long way. Even today, if somebody suggests something that sounds right, even if it's what we want to do, what we know we should do — because someone else said it, we won't.

The man went on to describe the effective antidote he had devised to curb his willful ways. "I am practicing actions that adapt to the rules," he said, "like fastening my seatbelt, which I always refused to do. Maybe following this rule will save my life. Maybe following all the rules will save my life in more ways than one."

I will listen to the wisdom of others and follow that wisdom when it sounds right to me.

October

*Others will mostly treat you the way
you treat yourself.*
— *Muhamed Moussa*

We set the rules as to how others see us and how we choose to be treated. Our self-image is what we project to others, and it is that image they respond to.

Just as the way we treat others is basically the way we treat ourselves, the way we see others, interpret their actions and words, is the way we see ourselves. If we are judgmental with others we are likely to be just as hard on ourselves, and vice versa.

Growing up in a dysfunctional family can be likened to a forge. Within a forge, white-hot metal is fashioned into an object for a specific purpose. All too often adult children have been "forged" to see themselves as flawed, imperfect, powerless people who have little say about what happens to them in life. This self-image invites a like response from others. As we learn to be different, we come to see ourselves as different, and others will respond to our proud, emerging new self.

I now see that I am largely responsible for my effect on others. I am learning to teach people how I would like to be treated.

October 2

When a man has pity on all living crea-
tures then only is he noble.
— *Buddha*

Sometimes our own difficulties seem so great we give little thought to the reality of other people's lives. When this happens we lose the ability to be compassionate.

Compassion is a lovely word that means literally to "suffer with others." Compassionate people are those who have room in their spirits to offer hospitality to others. They are, in a real sense, builders of spiritual houses where others can find safety and security on a cold bitter night.

The fact is, we are not the only ones who hurt. We are not the only ones with wounds. We are not the only people with stories. Every human being has a story. We all fight a difficult fight. The compassionate person understands this and is able to escape the sense of isolation that so often accompanies times of personal hardship. Compassion allows us to listen. In that listening, we see our own difficulties in a saner perspective. Compassion draws and joins us to others, and then everything makes better sense.

Today, I am aware that others are struggling too.

You can't be a good egg all your life —
you either have to hatch or go bad.
— Fr. Ralph Pfau

We must all take our turn at being followers until we're ready to lead. So, until that time, we follow by listening to others, doing as they do, leaning on their wisdom and experience.

Then the time comes for us to assume leadership. This is the point when we have heard most of what the others have to say, and received most of what the group has to give. By applying those principles and practices in our daily lives, we have become ready to take on a different role.

There will always be people who are just becoming aware of themselves as adult children. They will come to meetings hesitantly and be looking to us for comfort, direction, challenge, and wisdom. They give us our chance to share the gifts we've received. The quality of the leadership we have to offer is entirely dependent on our willingness and ability to take responsibility when the time comes.

Today, I will assess my progress in the program. I will not lose any opportunity to share what I have learned.

October 4

What reason weaves, by passion is un-
done.

— Alexander Pope

Self-esteem is always the result of self-image. As we see ourselves, so we place value on ourselves. Self-esteem is basically the value we place upon ourselves.

Self-image is the definition we have of ourselves. It is what we see when we look in the mirror of our own perceptions. Thus it is critical that we take care of the behaviors and situations we place ourselves in — for from these our definition of "self" is made.

Fruitlessly pursuing lost loves is self-defeating. Driving around an ex-lover's apartment at four in the morning, or checking out parking lots behind bars, or attempting to find true love in a singles bar, is simply self-defeating behavior. While we are engaged in any such behavior, the definition of ourselves as loser, as always suffering, as never having anything go right, is being deepened. Of course it is. We are setting up situations where that is the only possible consequence. We need to be aware of the consequences of our actions.

Today, I will consider the difference between obsession and love.

Ask, and ye shall receive, that your joy
may be full.

— *John 16:24*

Some profound thoughts, gems of wisdom that have endured for centuries, can make us angry and resentful. Depending on our experience, one idea can evoke a wide range of emotional response. The quote above, for example, might make a lot of people laugh, shudder, or scoff. Perhaps their life experience taught them not to ask because, whenever they did, they found rejection. So they learned not to ask.

But recovery is learning new truths. What recovering adult children learn is that who you ask is what makes the difference. We learn to stop taking our requests to untrustworthy people. When we do that, we discover that we will receive when we ask only those we can count on to be there for us.

There is interest, support, and positive reinforcement available to all of us in the program. All we need to do is ask the right people.

I will not make a virtue of giving trust to everyone. Trust must be earned. I will be discerning in who I trust and who I don't trust.

October 6

> *For many people, God is just Dad with*
> *a mask on.*
>
> — *Anonymous*

Establishing a loving relationship with God, as we understand God to be, is the core of the spiritual journey of recovery. In searching for a God we can understand, many of us adult children hit a brick wall. Our image of God as Father filters through our image of our human father.

When we think about God's will, what God wants for us, and what God wants of us, the answers we receive look surprisingly like the answers we'd get if we substituted Dad for God. And since many of us didn't have a very healthy relationship with Dad, we may feel very angry at God. But is it really God we're having trouble with, or is it deeply buried, convoluted feelings toward a male authority figure?

Once we're able to tell the difference, once we take the Dad-mask off God, we can start over, ask new questions, and test new possibilities with the God of our understanding.

Today, I will clearly discern which of my attitudes about God are rooted in my past relationship with my father and which are truly free to relate to God.

*For us, there is only the trying, the rest
is not our business.*
— *T. S. Eliot*

In nearly every endeavor of human existence it is
abundantly clear that achievement is only to be
gained at the cost of conscious, consistent effort.

Successful business people put meticulous detail
into the operation of their businesses. Marathon
runners daily extend themselves while keeping
close track of times, distances, and the subtle (or
not so subtle) messages their bodies send them.
Repeatedly, we have told our children some version of the truth, "If you are not willing to pay
your dues, you cannot expect success." The same is
true with the most important of all human
achievements: personal growth.

Yet when we look at the decimated effects of
growing up in a dysfunctional environment, more
often than not what we demand are instant rewards with little effort. Let us remember the marathon runner out slogging through the miles. We
must be willing to work if we are to win this most
important of all events.

*Knowing I'm not responsible for outcomes focuses
energy on the footwork for which I am responsible.*

October 8

I am an old man and have known many troubles, but most of them never happened.

— Mark Twain

Imagination is wonderful if we don't use it against ourselves. Like fire it is a reality of great power capable of either warming and giving life or of burning and destroying everything it touches. Consider how often we create problems that never come to be! Family gatherings we know will drive us crazy turn out to be uneventful or even pleasant. Phone calls we put off for months or years because of the excruciating pain they will cause are not the big deal we thought they would be. Once made, decisions we dreaded and avoided improve our lives so much that we wonder what we were waiting for!

We adult children often grow up wearing "doom glasses." Everything we see is filtered through those darkened lenses. How much of what we dread, fear, and run from is really more a figment of imagination, than fact. How much of our lives and energy do we spend on avoiding what does not yet exist and perhaps never will?

I am learning not to borrow trouble from the future.

Life is not war, and people are not the enemy.

— *Anonymous*

Some of us adult children have learned — by seeing it, hearing it, having it driven into our consciousness in a hundred ways — that life is indeed war. We were raised in families that *assumed* conflict and combat and thus delivered messages like, "This is going to be a terrible day. I can tell it already, and I haven't even left the house yet."

Some of us had homes that were veritable forts. We learned that we were only safe within the confines of the protected areas. Anyone not in there with us was an outsider, someone not to be trusted, an enemy.

But these are perceptions of truth — faulty perceptions — not truths themselves. The wars our parents fought were raging between their ears. It need not be so for us. Outsiders need not be the enemy unless we cast them in that role.

A contentious attitude always brings misery. We don't have to think that way if we don't want to.

I've learned that the expectation of hostility breeds hostility. Today, I expect nothing but pleasantness and peace.

October 10

Recovery is . . . Overcoming the fear of living.

— Anonymous

Many adult children live in constant fear — fear of both success and failure, fear of being alone and fear of being close to others, fear of living and fear of dying. Our heritage is fear.

It is a sure sign of recovery when we begin to see life as an exciting experience, an encounter of the best kind, rather than as a dangerous and terrifying venture into hostile territory. We know we are recovering when we can feel positive and curious about taking a small risk, when we can meet a new friend without being afraid of losing our identity, and when we can state our needs without sinking into a pit of guilt and fear.

Many situations in life are indeed terrifying. Awful things do happen to people. But it is just as true that life is full of sweetness and beauty. Recovery is admitting both and electing the latter.

Today, I will live as fully as I can, secure in the love of my Higher Power.

The easiest person to deceive is one's own seed.
— *Edward Bulwer-Lytton*

How much can we afford to lose? Of all the investments we might make, the most important and riskiest by far are in our personal relationships. Important because such investments put so much of our feelings, sense of self-worth, and serenity on the line. It is risky because the success of the relationship is so dependent on the other person's willingness and ability to play fair.

No matter how committed we are to making it work, if our partners don't have or won't do what it takes — we are out of luck. The quality of a relationship simply cannot be healthier than both of the parties involved.

It isn't cold or calculating to consider well the implications and ramifications of an important investment. It is fulfilling a primary responsibility to ourselves, to our partners, and to our Higher Power.

Today, I will examine my delusions about myself and the people I love: What's really going on here?

October 12

So often we search out the impossible
— and then throw ourselves into trying
to do it.

— Anonymous

If we have an inner rule that says we must fail, one way to obey this miserable directive is to take on only impossible tasks and then predicate our self-worth on the outcome.

Such tasks may be impossible by their very nature (as in changing someone who does not want to be changed), or by circumstance (as in attempting to accomplish a two-year project in a week), or by our lack of personal qualification (as in an all-thumbs person who insists on being a brain surgeon). Any of these tasks will be "successful" for us because we certainly will fail at them. And unless we've gotten some insight into the insanity of the old rules, the more impossible the task is, the harder we'll try to accomplish it.

There are no born losers. We all deserve to win. Let's be sure we're taking on our next task not because it can't be done, but because it can.

No matter what the old messages say, I will not set myself up for failure.

Be like the bird that, passing on her
flight awhile on boughs too slight, feels
them give way beneath her, and yet
sings, knowing that she hath wings.
— *Victor Hugo*

Security. Upon what do we base our security?

If we place the sensation of security upon some outside condition or upon a reality that can offer no security, then surely when the bough breaks we will fall to disaster.

Recovering people for half a century have found a Power greater than themselves, a Power at hand that becomes our "wings." Slowly, we learn that by turning over our lives to the care of God as we understand God, we are not alone nor left to the strength of ourselves.

There is enormous ability to enjoy life, and a true sense of freedom when we learn to place our security in this all-loving God. Then, as we encounter situations we cannot control, we will be able to trust that we will not be dashed to the ground.

I am made bolder and braver by the knowledge
that my Higher Power will not let me fall.

October 14

The strongest bulwark of authority is uniformity; the least divergence from it is the greatest crime.
— *Emma Goldman*

Some people and some values simply don't deserve our allegiance. But adult children frequently find it difficult to make such discriminations. Many of us have internalized a deep rule that demands unquestioning loyalty — in the sense that loyalty means we must not question or reject authority.

We tend to blindly submit to old rules even as adults. Without thinking, we automatically obey such rules as "Never cry," "Be seen and not heard," "Be perfect," and "Never bother anyone." Even though we know there's nothing wrong with crying or speaking up, that no one can be perfect, and that adults shouldn't worry about bothering other adults, we continue to do as we were told — perhaps 50 years ago!

A wise person doesn't automatically pledge loyalty to anyone or anything. Loyalty must be earned, and the voices that request our loyalty must be more than echoes reverberating down the halls of time.

Am I still obeying old rules that don't apply anymore? Today, I will make conscious, adult choices.

*Have patience with all things, but first
of all with yourself.*
                              — *Francis de Sales*

At times all of us are influenced by the prevailing societal demand: "Hurry up." We are surrounded by "instants," from instant potatoes to instant photographs. We consistently hear that faster is better — "My computer is better than yours because it now works in milliseconds." Thus, bewitched by this neurotic demand, we become incredibly impatient people. We sometimes hurry up so we can slow down. We rave at people driving too slowly for our taste. We berate a waitress for not attending to us quickly enough, thinking she is doing it on purpose when quite possibly it is just that her feet hurt.

And as with all habits, it becomes so routine we no longer even question the habit; it is simply normal. It becomes so much a part of us we are unable to even question it.

All great things take time. All genuine, precious growth takes time. Growth is not in the economy of milliseconds or hurry up. When we lose patience under the rush of going faster, we miss the vast amount of beauty surrounding us.

Today, I am peaceful in the knowledge that faster isn't better — better is better.

October 16

Courage is grace under pressure.
— *Ernest Hemingway*

Establishing a loving relationship with God, as we understand God to be, is the core of the spiritual journey of recovery. In searching for a God we can understand, many of us adult children hit a brick wall. Our image of God as Father filters through our image of our human father.

When we think about God's will, what God wants for us, and what God wants of us, the answers we receive look surprisingly like the answers we'd get if we substituted Dad for God. And since many of us didn't have a very healthy relationship with Dad, we may feel very angry at God. But is it really God we're having trouble with, or is it deeply buried, convoluted feelings toward a male authority figure?

Once we're able to tell the difference, once we take the Dad-mask off God, we can start over, ask new questions, and test new possibilities with the God of our understanding.

Today, I will clearly discern which of my attitudes about God are rooted in my past relationship with my father and which are truly free to relate to God.

*I could accept everybody else's vulnera-
bility — but not my own.*
— *Mae L.*

We've all heard it's more blessed to give than to
receive. Fewer of us have heard that receiving is
equally blessed and also a lot more difficult. Does
someone need our compassion, our time, our
money? Just ask us and we'll give it. Gift giving is
just our cup of tea. Oh, but to be on the receiving
end — that is another matter. To wholly accept a
love-gift is beyond many of us. Receiving is painful. It makes us nervous and suspicious. It makes
us feel vulnerable. We are strangers to the wisdom
that receiving is the deepest form of giving.

Authentic love not only forgives the vulnerability and mistakes of others, but receives that forgiveness. To wholly accept forgiveness means we
can't go around flogging ourselves for our mistakes
and failures. We have to let it go and receive the
truth that we are pardoned.

To receive the love of others is to remove the
mask of perfection, and forgive ourselves for being
human.

*Today, I will examine my behavior as a receiver as
well as a giver of love.*

October 18

Fatigue makes cowards of us all.
— Vince Lombardi

Sometimes we just feel like pulling the covers up over our heads. We're tired of hanging on and afraid of letting go. We're tired of putting ourselves on the line, feeling vulnerable, taking risks. Our progress seems stalled; compared to us, snails move along like racehorses.

At these times it's a good idea to pull back and rest for a while. We need to remember that frustration and disappointment are inevitable elements of the journey, the thorns that come with the roses. We must not expect it to be otherwise. Of course we'll get too tired sometimes. The path to recovery runs uphill, and it is littered with stumbling blocks. Climbing isn't cakewalking; we've earned our exhaustion and deserve a rest when we need it. It is simply old "stinking thinking" to decide we don't, or shouldn't, need a rest. It is old behavior to feel guilty about resting. Tomorrow is another day. Tomorrow we'll be refreshed and ready to move again.

Today, I will practice giving myself a break when I need it. I will give myself the same consideration I would give any other weary traveler.

A wrongdoer is often a man that has left something undone, not always he that has done something.
— Marcus Aurelius

Some of us have felt so wronged for so long that it's hard to even imagine ourselves on the other end of the pointed stick. We're so conditioned to the victim's role we have a hard time recognizing our own aggression. But many of us play both roles, whether actively or passively, directly or indirectly. We all have apologies to make.

Because we've chronically thought of ourselves as being owed rather than owing apologies, we're not very skillful at asking for forgiveness. The simple words, "I'm sorry. I was wrong," don't come easily. More than others, we may tend to justify our wrongs because of all the wrongs that have been done to us. But it is essential to recovery that we learn to take responsibility when we have hurt other people. By promptly and honestly admitting our mistakes, we exercise healthy humility and knock down another barrier between ourselves and the rest of humanity. Withheld apologies are unpaid debts. Paying our debts is not a matter of weakness — it's a clear-cut matter of responsibility.

I am accountable both for what I do and for what I fail to do.

October 20

Forgiveness is a process.
                                    — Hulbert L.

Sometimes we think of forgiveness as an all-or-nothing kind of thing — once done, forever done. But forgiveness is most often a process that we make progress in one step at a time.

Willing is not the same as wanting. We may be willing to forgive but not want to. The injury done us may be so painful and fill us with such rage that forgiveness just can't be all-or-nothing. What we can do, however, is start. We can start thinking one forgiving thought a day. We can resist one hateful, resentful thought a day. We can continue further by acting out, however small that action may be, a forgiving action every day. The process can continue as we make a list of all the reasons why not forgiving is hurting us more than it hurts others. It can go on as we learn to pray for those we are trying to forgive.

All of a sudden we will find that the unattainable forgiveness has been accomplished. But of course it wasn't all of a sudden at all.

Today, I pray for courage to begin the process of forgiveness and faith to believe in it.

*We have too many high sounding
words, and too few actions that corres-
pond with them.*
— *Abigail Adams*

There are many recurring themes and phrases in
the conversations of recovering people. One of
these catchy capsules of wisdom is, *to try to is to
lie to.* What this means is that we are tempted to
use words as a smokescreen for our actions.

But words, of course, are never an adequate substitute for action. Because we are human, and
therefore subject to fear and fatigue, we sometimes
tend to alibi by saying we tried to do something we
should have in fact done. We tried to talk straight,
or we tried to confront a bully, when we know we
really didn't make the effort. As the phrase says,
we are simply lying when we claim to have done
something we didn't do.

And it isn't necessary to lie. If we're not up to
making an effort we need to say, "I can't handle
that today. Maybe tomorrow." We need to be honest more than we need to look good.

*I don't need to justify my behavior to myself or
anyone else. No matter what words I use — the
truth is the truth.*

October 22

Some circumstantial evidence is very strong, as when you find a trout in the milk.

— Henry David Thoreau

There are many things adult children may not remember or want to remember, but the circumstantial evidence of what happened back then stands out clearly. Admitting those past events may be the only way we can leave them in the past instead of dragging them around with us.

If we find it nearly impossible to be good to ourselves, we probably learned long ago we didn't deserve to be treated well. If we repeatedly fall into dependent relationships, this may be proof that we learned to get validity only in our relationships to other people. To have learned self-defeating attitudes doesn't mean our teachers were evil. It does mean, however, that we learned what they had to teach. The evidence is too strong to deny. The consequences are too important to ignore.

I resolve to accept the truth. Admitting there was trauma in my past does not mean my past was filled with evil people.

No rule of recovery will work if I don't.
— Iris S.

It's quite possible to confuse getting ready to recover with actually doing the work that results in recovery. All the reading we do, the meetings we attend, and the sharing with others can still be just "getting ready."

Recovery begins after we've gathered information, talked about it, thought about it, and written about it. Recovery is doing, acting, working. The work of recovery is in progress if we actually say "no" when "no" needs to be said, when we stay put when old tapes tell us to run, when we let ourselves get good and angry when we are tempted to deny that a situation is outrageous.

The work of getting ready is still work however. Such work is not to be slighted. Each "getting ready" activity we do takes us inch by inch to the spiritual jumping off point where we are ready to confront the demons in our lives.

Recovery comes to be when we actually stand up, dig down, and face off the old destructive patterns that hold us captive.

Today, I will be aware that thinking about doing is not the same as doing. Today, I will act.

October 24

> *The race is not to the swift, nor the*
> *battle to the strong.*
>
> — *Ecclesiastes*

Overwhelming firepower doesn't win most battles — especially battles of the inner kind — but patience and persistence do.

We adult children have many battles to fight. Battles with negative thinking, male or female dependency, fear of abandonment, shame, and guilt. We often feel weak, unsure, and powerless against such terrifying and constant forces.

When we think we can't put up a fight one more day, we need to remember that we learned these attitudes one day at a time, event by event, thought by thought. And that's the only way we can beat them — one blow at a time.

Patience and persistence must be our secret weapons. Homely and undramatic as they are, these two inner soldiers will advance the struggle far more than an exhausting frontal assault that may rage momentarily and then die out.

I am confident that patience and persistence will win out in the long run. And I am grateful for that insight.

To affirm life is to deepen, to make more inward, and to exalt the will to live.

— *Albert Schweitzer*

Not even the meanest circumstances can make us jealous, self-pitying, or greedy unless we allow them to. While we can't control all our experiences, we can control our responses. Unless we refuse the responsibility, we are in charge of our own reactions.

Consider, for example:

On the same street we can meet a man with no legs who is happily, serenely going about his business, and another man who is cursing fate because his shoes are tight. We can meet a peaceful, contented old woman who has known nothing but poverty, and a well-educated, beautifully dressed young woman who is depressed because she can't afford a new car. We can meet the drunken alcoholic slumped in a doorway and his recovering brother laughing with a group of friends after an A.A. meeting.

We, all of us, can learn to live above our circumstances if we're willing to alter our attitudes.

I am the master of my own reactions. Today, I choose to enjoy the roses in spite of the thorns.

October 26

*We make a living by what we get. We
make a life by what we give.*
— *Paula L.*

Many of us adult children think and feel we
have nothing to give. Our self-image is so stuck in
low self-esteem that we hide from others rather
than seek others out, we repress our ideas and
opinions rather than express them, we discount
our own experience as unworthy of anyone's interest or profit.

But the quality of our lives is determined by the
gifts we give. And we do have gifts — gifts that no
one else can give. Who understands the binding
power of shame better than we do? Who can reach
out with more compassion to newcomers who are
convinced they are flawed to the core? We can turn
the straw of our failed relationships into gold by
befriending those who haven't learned yet, as we
have learned, how to break the destructive cycle of
failure feeding upon failure. We're safe; we *know*.

Our gifts are precious beyond price. If we are
willing to give them, we can change the world.

*Today, I will stand proud and tall as one who has
riches to share.*

Continued to take personal inventory and when we were wrong promptly admitted it.

— Step Ten of
Alcoholics Anonymous

The Tenth Step wisely exhorts us to take a stitch before the whole seam is gone, to fix the leaky faucet before we have a flood, to keep checking the oil level to protect the engine from damage. The Tenth is the taking-care-of-business Step.

There's nothing fun or exciting about maintenance. While it's essential to ongoing well-being, it can seem tedious and annoying to reflect back on each day with a critical eye. And we don't enjoy repeatedly seeking out and admitting our faults. But the discipline of a daily Tenth Step is the best precaution we can take to safeguard our gains and prevent further losses.

Like a mirror, a daily Tenth Step gives us a clear, realistic picture — not one distorted by despair or wishful thinking — of who we are and how we're doing. And, just as we use a mirror, we need only check ourselves out and go along with our business. A Tenth Step only takes a minute or two.

I am grateful to have an effective tool to keep myself on track.

October 28

> *Treat all things as if they were loaned to you without any ownership — whether body or soul, sense or strength, external goods or honors, house or hall . . . everything.*
>
> — *Meister Eckhart*

Just because we can't afford jewels and antiques doesn't mean we aren't posessive. *Mine* is the dearest word and concept of some of us who barely get by from paycheck to paycheck: *my* car, *my* house, *my* savings account, *my* children, *my* husband — even *my* alcoholic!

Yet ownership, particularly of other people, is really a delusion of control. The mistaken notion that someone is ours breeds anxiety, a misplaced sense of responsibility, and an exaggerated fear of loss. At most, we can only be stewards of our relationships, let alone our belongings.

Something wonderful happens as we practice thinking of the people we love as being on loan. Instead of insisting that they must be with us always, we can enjoy the pleasure of their company today. We can open our hands and give them and us the space to discover the joy of living freely.

Today, I will make a start at letting go.

*Watch ye, stand fast in the faith, quit
you like a man, be strong.*
— *I Corinthians*

The concept of problem ownership has brought great relief to many of us adult children. But often, even when we've turned over the problem, we still have the pain. In fact, the problem may well be theirs, but the pain is still ours.

Inevitably, going forward is painful. We may have to move away from people, systems, and places that, however toxic, are still part of us. Some of these were us — our personal, private history. There are no two ways about it — leave-taking hurts.

But everything is hard before it gets easy. New attitudes and actions will not always be uncomfortable. It's okay to hurt for a while. Let us be patient, remembering that pain passes as recovery progresses.

Only the dead have no pain in their lives. Today, I am grateful for life and breath and opportunity.

October 30

There's no art to find the mind's construction in the face.
        — William Shakespeare

Babies' faces are wonderful — not only because they're physically beautiful, but because they're absolutely candid. It is a rarity and a joy to look into a face that pretends nothing, hides nothing, and disguises nothing. Such faces are beautiful because they reveal wholeness.

Few adults have such faces. And, unlike babies, who are innocent because they lack experience and are yet untouched, adults may be survivors of brutal experience.

For some adults, candor and openness have been reborn because they were willing, over time, to abandon their masks one by one. Now that they aren't hiding anything, they don't have to prevent anyone from looking in. Because their insides match their outsides, their faces clearly reflect the wholeness that was restored to them. It is a privilege as well as a joy to see such clarity and freshness shining out of an adult human being. And it is evidence that renewal is possible.

Personal renewal is possible for me; my program promises it.

Being is more important than doing.
        — Betty Lou B.

Reflection is important, but difficult. Meditation and reflection may seem almost impossible to some of us because these activities involve "doing" nothing. We cling to the belief that achievement, success, and progress mean doing something.

One myth in our society is that people who produce are worthwhile and people who don't are worthless. Without reflection, we tend to buy that idea whole. We don't examine or even wonder about the implications until something happens to our personal lives to drive home the foolishness of that idea: If we have a retarded child or become physically disabled or retire, what do we do then? We continue to live. And that is sufficient. Life, like beauty, is its own reason for being.

It's too bad we have to learn so many things the hard way. "Doing" is important, of course, but doing isn't everything. Being and doing are not the same thing: being is first and foremost.

Today, I will take time for reflection. I will question the importance of some of my "busy-ness."

November

Whether you think you can or whether
you think you can't — you are right.
                    — Henry Ford

Attitude shapes the quality of our lives. If we perceive ourselves as failures, as helpless victims who are only kidding ourselves with all this talk of recovery — and if that attitude is not contested — then truly, we are not capable of change.

If, on the other hand, our attitude is positive, a whole new set of realities emerges. Empowered by a different self-perception, we see that our lives are largely of our own making, that the past does not have to rule us like a tyrant king, that we are more able than we ever dreamed, and that indeed we are capable of deciding anew who we will be and how we will live.

Reality itself only rarely determines outcomes. Our attitude toward that reality is what makes the difference. People in general are limited by attitude, not by opportunity. What one person judges to be a miserable, rainy day may be to another a marvelous opportunity to sell umbrellas.

I am responsible for my own world view. I — not others — choose the kind of glasses I'm going to wear.

November 2

> *Give a little love to a child and you get*
> *a great deal back.*
> — *John Ruskin*

Many of us are scared to death of the wounded child living within us. We're afraid of remembering too much, afraid of feeling overwhelmed, afraid of the rage that will be stirred up. But in spite of all that learned fear, there is good reason to listen to what that precious part of us has to say.

Children, no matter how wounded, are naturally honest. Play is their main task in life. Wonder, imagination, trust, and love are as much a part of them as their fingers and toes. The very young haven't had time yet to practice the deadly skill of deceit.

Our child is still there — within. That child still speaks messages of innocence and still waits to be heard and acknowledged. It is the child within, although it may be wounded, that waits to teach us and lead us along the road to recovery. Often the child leads the adult to wisdom.

As I become stronger, I am more willing and able than I used to be to spend time with my inner child.

Someone has said that the greatest cause of ulcers is mountain-climbing over molehills.

— Maxwell Maltz

Every problem that arises doesn't qualify as a crisis. And in spite of our tendency to overreact, every crisis that confronts us isn't necessarily a do-or-die situation. Rather than shrink in fear or attack in anger, we can take a more reasoned, measured approach by evaluating the difficult situations that come up before we respond.

How important is it? A misunderstanding between friends, for example, is not the end of the world. Whose problem is it? If one of our children gets a bad grade at school, the responsibility lies with that child, not with us. Overreaction is inappropriate in either case.

When we do face a true crisis, when an important decision has to be made, we need all our wisdom and ability to focus the strength of our program on making a good choice. We won't have the energy or perspective to do that unless we can tell the difference between molehills and mountains.

Today, I will see circumstances as they are — without minimizing or exaggerating.

November 4

When you've said it the best you can,
you've said it the best you can.
> — *Tim U.*

There's only so much we can do to help other people, or a certain other person, understand us. Beyond that, our best efforts are wasted. Especially if the other person doesn't *want* to understand. It is impossible to communicate with someone who cannot or will not communicate with us. The communication problem doesn't always lie with us; it may lie with others who choose not to listen. We are responsible for communicating our thoughts and feelings as clearly as we can. But we are not responsible for the other person's interpretation of our message. We've done our part when we've honestly said what we have to say. If the other person won't accept it, or feels hurt, confused, or angry, we are not responsible. And we are not obliged to endlessly keep on trying to explain ourselves.

Other people's refusal to hear is not our problem — it's theirs. Sincere seekers of understanding will find it.

Today, I will not be frustrated by someone else's unwillingness to communicate. I will accept what is.

It's hard for the modern generation to understand Thoreau, who lived beside a pond but didn't own water skis or a snorkel.

— *Bill Vaughn*

Young people think they know so many things that youth and inexperience simply cannot know. Remember, for example, all the things we were so sure we'd never do as adults: "I'll never hound my kids about homework like my mom does," "I'll always stay in shape," "I'll never fall asleep in front of the TV like my dad," "When *I* get a good job, I won't be stingy with my money like my parents are," "I'll never get so uptight that I make a big screaming deal about a few wet towels on the floor."

Until the reality of the years overtakes us, we imagine that we are too vital and too smart for adjustments, compromises, or failure. Lots of us who vowed we would never be unavailable to our kids became dysfunctional ourselves. In spite of our assumption of superiority, our turn came and "we" became "they."

Recognizing the pattern should give us a better understanding of both ends of the spectrum.

I am becoming less judgmental as I realize that we are all traveling the same path.

November 6

Work will win. Wishing won't.
— Ed B.

There is a time and a place for everything — wishing is one of them. Sometimes it is extremely therapeutic (to say nothing of just fun) to wish upon a star. In those moments, we can conjure up the most delicious situations and events. These may well become road maps to reality at some point.

There are times, however, when wishing is not sufficient. There are times when the only appropriate response is work. There are times when all the wishing in the world will not do the work that needs to be done. Wishing alone does not get us to meetings or accomplish the important insights gained from actually sitting down and working through our family of origin situations. Wishing alone does not let go of resentments, start relationships, or improve our physical conditioning.

There is a time for both. Wishing and work are both benevolent. Our task is to know the difference between the two and decide one is called for and not the other.

The different purposes of wishing and doing are becoming clearer to me.

> *He has the right to criticize who has the*
> *heart to help.*
> — *Abraham Lincoln*

Looking back we can find much in our past to criticize, to be unhappy about. That attitude can, all too often and too easily, become pointed toward the future. Before an event has even happened we can find much to criticize, to be glum about, to find fault with.

The issue is very much in the attitude. Whether we are looking backward or forward or simply around us in the here and now, it is our attitude that interprets what we see.

When we're willing to correct what is wrong and fix what is broken, the criticizing becomes much more constructive; it becomes an effort to identify what needs to be done instead of a lament that nothing can be done. Much of what recovery is about can be done. We have it within our power to make many changes affecting the quality of our lives.

Today, I won't challenge anyone else's behavior unless I'm also willing to be part of the solution.

November 8

> *Let us then be up and doing,*
> *With a heart for any fate,*
> *Still achieving, still pursuing,*
> *Learn to labor and to wait.*
> *— Henry Wadsworth Longfellow*

A master sculptor may strike a block of marble a hundred times before anything noticeable happens. Yet the hundred-and-first blow creates a perfect break in the stone. What caused the perfect break — the last blow or the hundred that went before?

So it is with personal growth. We may see no appreciable gain made by a long series of consistent, dogged efforts. And then it happens. All of a sudden a corner is turned, a truth is revealed, a bad habit loses it grip.

But of course it didn't happen suddenly. The gain was made, one blow at a time, one step at a time, by all the seemingly ineffective, probably forgotten efforts that preceded the turn around.

Today, I have absolute faith in the process of growth. I no longer expect a medal for each lap run.

Be suspicious of substitutes.
                        — *Connie L.*

When something important is missing in our lives, our natural tendency is to scramble around until we find something, anything in an attempt to fill the gap. We may use food, alcohol, money, sex — anything. That's how addictions begin: We don't know how to get what we need, so we reach for something else. What we are often reaching for in these "switched addictions" is love and acceptance. Addictions do not generate love but only the illusion of love.

Substitutes make us sick. Even if they're not bad in themselves, we abuse them. We forget they're alternatives and stopgaps rather than the real thing.

Sometimes we don't know what our real needs are. And sometimes we do know, but we're afraid to take the risks involved in meeting them. In either case, we will continue to be slaves to our addictions or substitutions until we recognize them for what they are and learn to satisfy our needs in healthy ways.

Today, I will ask my Higher Power for insights about my real needs. I will check out my life for substitutes.

November 10

A man of courage is also full of faith.
— *Cicero*

Faith and courage walk hand in hand. Courage empowers us to act in favor of what we believe, but cannot know. Courage is animated by the vision of faith. It doesn't take any faith to perform an action that doesn't require a risk. Only when the outcome is uncertain, and the effort itself a feat of daring, must faith and courage come on the scene together to get the job done.

To reach out to another, if we have known frequent rejection, is to act courageously in spite of an uncertain outcome. To stand firm in a decision, if we have always given in and given up, is to back our faith in a most daring and courageous way.

Many recovering people, who never think of themselves as spiritual, are excellent models of faith because they continually reach out for what is not common in their lives. Because they believe, they're willing and able to take the risk.

Today, I can do what I believe I can do.

All is well that ends well.
> — *John Heywood*

It has been said, "In the game of life nothing is less important than the score at halftime." Halftime means it is not over; the game is still in progress, and the outcome is still not decided.

It would be wonderful if all people started out with families steeped in relational skills and who knew how to listen, care, and encourage. Many, however, did not start out that way.

All of which simply means it is only halftime. The final score has not been posted. The quality of our lives is determined not by how we start but by how we shall choose to end. We can learn the skills necessary for a successful life whether we start with them or not. We can learn to care about ourselves and others, to stand firm in our relationships, and to choose wisely. Who we were was given; who we shall be is up to us.

I now see each new day as another chance for growth and happiness. From this day forward, I am in charge of the quality of my life.

November 12

The worst loneliness is not to be comfortable with yourself.

— Mark Twain

We all strive to escape loneliness, especially if that sense of being isolated is more or less constant. Sometimes in response to that fear we become dependent on others; we generate nonstop movement or noise just so we don't have to be alone.

Who are we running from?

There is enormous joy in discovering that when we're alone we have ourselves as company. We come to like ourselves and discover the word "us" is sweet indeed. We're not perfect or necessarily sweeter than anyone else, but we are just fine. We can learn to look forward to our thoughts and not run from them in fear. We can even learn to look gently into the mirror and find our best friend there. The more we come to understand that, the less we fear the quiet. In fact, there will come many times when we consciously seek quiet and aloneness. When we cease being afraid of ourselves, we find freedom from most of the fears of life.

I am growing more able to find peace and enjoyment in my own company.

*Events of great consequence often
spring from trifling circumstances.*
— *Livy*

For people committed to recovery, almost any
event, no matter how commonplace or small, can
be an exciting opportunity for personal growth.
The trick is to recognize the opportunity.

One little smile, if mustered by a shy, fearful
person, may set in motion a series of positive
events that have life-changing consequences. Telling a simple truth, when exaggerating or lying has
been the rule, may signal a major breakthrough.
Many adult children have learned never to take a
risk, but risks allow us to set course for a new and
better shore. Some of us find it infinitely easier to
say it doesn't matter when it really does. Reasonable risk is a major step forward no matter how
small the assertive comment may seem. When do
opportunities for growth occur? Any time and all
the time.

If we're looking, we'll find many chances to
springboard ourselves toward a new way of being.
All it takes is a start. Even the smallest effort will
do.

*I will not miss a chance to start building new
habits this day. Time counts and I will not miss
any opportunity.*

November 14

One conviction is worth 99 opinions.
— Mitch G.

Confidence and certitude are the best gifts we can give to newcomers. They need to hear they are indeed wonderful people, of course there is hope and help, and certainly they deserve happiness and serenity.

On the early road to recovery, many of us were without these strong convictions. We had only long-held opinions, and most of them were negative. We may have begun our program burdened by a self-image that told us we were not intelligent, not attractive, and generally without value.

What a surprise and a boost to meet people who saw us differently! Here were people who believed that we were "tens" and could help us see it, too. Eventually, our negative opinions proved no match for the conviction they taught us to share.

We CAN make a difference in people's lives. The image of themselves we reflect back to them may become the cornerstone of a brave new conviction. Pass it on.

Today, I will share what I have. I will throw my weight against negative opinions.

*The way to be most helpful to others is
to do what would be most helpful to
myself.*
— *Catherine Burford North*

One of our neurotic rules is that we must be
responsible for the health, wealth, and happiness
of other people. As we obey this rule through the
years, "What must I do for others?" often becomes
the consuming question of our lives.

But we can only give what we have to give —
which is ourselves. Compulsive, slavish service is
not a gift; it's a conditioned response to life. Trying
to buy love with presents we can't afford is irresponsibility, not generosity.

Strange as it may sound, our own mental health
is no doubt the greatest gift we can give anybody.
Which means that if we really want to do our
loved ones a favor, we will take care of ourselves.

And who knows? We may be just the expression
of sanity and recovery needed to inspire someone
else.

*Today, I pray to fully understand the old adage,
"Charity begins at home." I acknowledge my need
for my own charity.*

November 16

> *When I am anxious it is because I am living in the future. When I am depressed it is because I am living in the past.*
>
> — *Jimmy R.*

Like many words of wisdom, the truth behind this thought is a lot easier to agree with than it is to live with. The everyday reality is that we do tend to be anxious when we're trying to be responsible for all the projects on our list. It's easy to go too far — to worry about bills that aren't due yet, events planned for months in the future, disasters that may or may not happen.

And it's easy to spend too much time rummaging around in the closet of our memories. Opportunities lost years ago, promising relationships that almost (but didn't) work out, real or imagined rejections — these can all be dragged out of the closet and made to dance on the stage of our consciousness.

What about right now? Is the sun shining today? Are we healthy? Are we free to move around and shake things up?

My healthy choice today is to live these twenty-four hours as a bright potential untarnished by yesterday.

An excuse is a lie guarded.
— *Jonathan Swift*

Delusion is the blindfold we wear to our own execution. We can spend too much of our lives rationalizing irresponsible behavior and making alibis. For some of us delusion has become a habit. Making excuses for our negative behaviors has too often become second nature.

Like a bad penny, delusion will keep popping up. We need to watch out for it, to be alert to thoughts such as these: "Maybe I just drank because of all the problems I had then. Those problems are gone now — I bet I could try it again." Or how about this? "We've both changed. Maybe I was too hard on him. Maybe he won't be abusive this time. I think I've learned to handle him better."

The blindness of delusion has cost us too much already. We need to be on guard. The more we practice making healthy decisions the more we will learn to trust our intuition, take risks, and leave unhealthy relationships and patterns behind. Bad habits are all we have to lose.

I can guard against self-delusion and be honest with myself and others.

November 18

*When I became a man, I put away
childish things.*

— I Corinthians

There is a difference in the way children and
adults solve problems. When adults lose something they tend to think, "Now where did I leave
that thing?"

A child who loses a toy tends to immediately go
back to the toy box where toys are supposed to be.
Children tend to return to the most familiar and
obvious place for answers.

The person sharing these ideas said he always
went back to his "toy box" when situations came
up that caused him fear or concern. These situations occurred when it came to giving in or standing up for himself, or to questions about relationships, or to giving himself a break, or any of the
complex situations that make adult children feel
nervous and insecure.

But in our "toy box," that childhood environment, we found most of the wrong answers to the
questions in the first place. Like the man who
shared, we need to find new answers, new sources
of information, new toys to play with.

*I have learned not to look for new answers in old
places. I'm better able to think before I act.*

Persistence is the master virtue. Without it, there is no other.

— Carol L.

How brave we are before the battle begins! Our helmets are shiny, our horses fresh, and our hearts filled with confidence. Woe to our enemies! Then the battle begins. How quickly visions of glory give way to the gritty realities of combat!

So it goes with the battles in our everyday lives. At first, going back to school seems thrilling — we can hardly wait to begin. Then we are behind in our reading, we didn't get a good grade on a test, and we'd rather stay home and watch TV than trudge off to class. It's the same with all our personal campaigns: the new diet gets boring fast, the fire and energy we brought to our first exercise class are difficult to come up with when our muscles are aching.

Just about everybody has the heart to begin a project. Persisting with it is another matter. In our case, the victory goes not to the smartest, the biggest, the wealthiest — but to the one who persists in spite of all.

Today, I pray for the strength to persevere when a task has stopped being fun.

November 20

*When men are full of envy they dispar-
age everything, whether it be good or
bad.*

— *Tacitus*

Envy is like a moth that gnaws slowly away
until the garment is ruined. The sad thing is that
envy damages, not an easily replaceable coat or
sweater, but our lives.

In what ways does envy hurt us? It makes us
cynical, for one thing. Nothing can be satisfying,
once we are riddled with envy. No one can be on
the level, nor can such things as honor, altruism,
or just plain friendship be accepted as real and
possible.

A chronically envious person has difficulty
maintaining friendships. There is too much pain in
closeness. Envious people need distance to protect
themselves and, because of this need, they are often alone and lonely.

The program offers us a lifetime of gifts — each
one with our name on it. "What we have coming"
is better than we can imagine. Envy damages our
ability to come into our own.

*My eyes are on my own goal. Today, I will be
satisfied to run my own race and sing my own
song.*

They are good, they are bad,
They are weak, they are strong,
They are wise, they are foolish — so
am I.

— *Sam Walters Foss*

We're not so different as we sometimes think. The fact is that almost everyone is an adult child in some way. The "they" we often position ourselves against, the supposed normal people we may both admire and envy, are in reality all of us. Do we know more than they do? Are they healthier than we are? Are they better than we are? Who is more deserving — them? Or us? There are no correct answers to such questions.

In given situations, we all have been good and bad, weak and strong, wise and foolish. Countless situations, none of them alcohol-related, have created emotional havoc in family life. The children of these homes grew up just as unevenly as we did. They, too, have their stories, their scars, and their brave hopes. They try and fail and try again, just as we do. They are just as imperfect as we are — and just as glorious.

As I regain perspective, I feel a new oneness with the rest of the human race.

November 22

> *Come, ye thankful people, come,*
> *Raise the song of Harvest-home;*
> *All is safely gathered in,*
> *Ere the winter storms begin.*
> — *Henry Alford*

Those who celebrated the first Thanksgiving were isolated, needy people who barely had a toe-hold in a strange land. They knew the battle was just beginning, that they were looking down the long barrel of a bitter winter.

They didn't wait to give thanks until they had won. They gave thanks for the success of survival; they were still alive. They gave thanks for the possibility of what could be, not that they had been spared enormous suffering and effort, because they hadn't.

As we sit in our easy chairs, smell the turkey roasting in our self-cleaning ovens, and wait for the football game on television, we might meditate for a few minutes on the original Thanksgiving. It may put us in touch with the true spirit of the day.

Today, I give thanks for the chance to give thanks.

*Recovery is civil war, but it is a war
that can be won.*

— *Sister Imelda*

How often do we hear people say, "Sure, I know
it's the right thing to do — but it's easier said than
done!" But "it," whatever "it" is for each of us, is
also easier done than not done. As hard as it is to
turn our will and our behavior toward recovery,
failing to recover is much harder. Ultimately, any
price we pay for recovery is far less than the cost of
giving up everything we've gained.

Some of us have a very difficult time making
phone calls. Others are scared to death of speaking
at meetings, talking to strangers, or admitting that
we have feelings. But the alternative has simply
been too painful. Whatever we have to do is worth
it. The payoff is immense. How many of us, when
we *did* attend that meeting that frightened us, felt
an enormous surge of self-confidence and happiness? How often, when we have stood our ground
and found it did not kill us, have we felt that we
could lick the world? The payoff is that we learn to
like ourselves more and that is as good as it gets.

*I will make sure today I am not forgetting the bene-
fits of recovery and only considering the price of
recovery.*

When we lose God, it is not God who
is lost.

— *Anonymous*

At times any of us can fall into the trap of trying to make deals with God. The thought seems to be, if I can make a deal with God then I can control the outcome that God alone seems to determine.

We cannot make deals with God — not because God is so hard-nosed, but because we don't need to bargain with God. The good we are trying to bargain for is already precious in the mind of God. We don't need to bargain for the benefit of others because God already loves those people and wants only good for them.

Yet at times we hear ourselves or others say things like, "Why doesn't God come through for me? I put my money in the offering tray every week, and I do things for my neighbors and friends. I volunteer for good causes. Yet I still feel insecure and scared. Why doesn't God answer my prayers?"

Perhaps the task is not to overwhelm God with all our effort but to quietly listen and discover the gift was outside our door all the time. We were just too busy to pick it up.

Today, I will be open to fresh insights about the God of my understanding.

*If we take care of the inches we will not
have to worry about the miles.*
— *Hartley Coleridge*

The elements of a program of recovery are like
many small stones tucked around the base of a
boulder. By itself, no one stone could hold the
boulder in place. But together, the stones ensure
that the boulder won't tear loose and come rampaging down the hill. The boulder represents all
the forces of destruction in our lives — the crippling experiences, the bad habits, the weak spots.
The task of the stones, which represent meetings,
daily reading, prayer, and practice of the Steps, is
to keep the boulder from destroying all that has
been built.

We pull out stones when we lose interest in
prayer, stop sharing, or get "too busy" to go to
meetings. Each stone we remove weakens the boulder's foundation until disaster is a matter of when,
not if. When the day of the big crash comes, will
we be surprised and resentful? Will we remember
that we were the ones who removed the stones? Or
will we blame it on someone else, bad luck, or
God?

*Today, I will keep close watch on the small stones
of my program.*

November 26

My family history begins with me.
— Plutarch

Holidays nearly always conjure up in our minds, and in the universal eyes, the myth of the media family. We are flooded with pictures of family reunions, warm family gatherings, people on their way home for the holidays.

Perhaps we have no such home. Perhaps we never did. It may well be that all the attention paid to home and family at this time of year serves to cause us much pain rather than joy.

Let us never forget that families and homes come in all manners and forms. Some of the best families are not biological. They are not the environment of love that was given us but those that we chose. We may find that the reality of family and home loving is indeed possible if we are willing to choose our family. It may be necessary to deliberately choose to surround ourselves with those who love and care for us. They are there. As many people are looking for family as we are. And with them we can experience warmth and acceptance.

As I develop my relationship skills, a family of loving hearts creates itself around me.

Henceforth I ask not good fortune,
I myself am good fortune.
— *Walt Whitman*

In having to grow up early and fast, many of us adult children actually functioned as "parents" to our parents. We saw our survival as dependent on taking care of everyone around us. In our desperate attempt to be "little adults" we missed out on being little children. But who said that couldn't be turned around?

Now that we are grown, we may have to struggle to learn to play. While it may be too late to play with dolls or put on a circus in the backyard, it is never too late to fly a kite on a pretty day, gather seashells, take a long bubble bath, or lie down on a blanket in the park and look for pictures in the clouds. And it is not too late to consciously invite the hurt child within us to come along for the adventures we plan. Tell your child that he or she is permanently off duty, that you will be the parent now, and that no one ever dreamed of the kind of good times that the two of you are going to have!

I am free to find joy and laughter. Today, I will discover them in my places.

November 28

*Sought through prayer and meditation
to improve our conscious contact with
God as we understood Him, praying
only for knowledge of His will for us
and the power to carry that out.*
— *Step Eleven of*
Alcoholics Anonymous

Be with me. That's what the Eleventh Step
sounds like. "Take my hand. Give me strength for
today's climb. Protect me from rock slides of self-
pity. Help me get up if I should stumble. Keep your
eye on me. I'm with you."

This is one person's example of daily, deliberate
contact with God as she understands God to be.
She thinks of her daily Eleventh Step as an invitation issued — a request for both leadership and
companionship. She finds healing, power, and
peace in the consistent practice of this Step. And
she doesn't have to walk alone through any of her
days. She travels in good company, with a friend
who knows the way.

There is order and stability in the universe. And
it is available to those who seek it. The Eleventh
Step keeps us going in the right direction.

*Knowing that I have God's constant companion-
ship fills my heart with joy.*

Me? I'm not angry about anything.
— *Karen F.*

The word *anger* doesn't begin to describe the absolute fury that festers in the hearts of adult children. There probably *is* no word, in fact, to capture the depth of what we feel. But that inner rage is a potent force in our lives, not the least because it is so deeply ingrained as to be invisible. Most of us wouldn't guess it was there if it weren't for the consequences.

Chronic, buried anger often causes dysfunctional behavior. One example is the hair-trigger, hothead reaction to almost anything — a flat tire, a cross word, a child's mistake. Petty slights are an outrage, minor inconveniences are intolerable. Extreme emotionlessness is another expression of repressed rage. Here we get the deadly silent treatment, the unwillingness or inability to respond. Then there are those of us who are simply scared to death of anger in any form and for any reason. Ours is the peace-at-any-price, don't-rock-the-boat reaction.

The question isn't whether we're angry or not. The question is whether or not we're dealing with it.

Today, I will express the anger I feel to my Higher Power and another human being.

November 30

Every man is his own chief enemy.
— Anacharsis

What would we think of people who threw litter on their own front lawns, poured a few cups of sugar in their gas tanks, and then splashed some catsup on their clothes before going to the big interview? Would we say that such behavior is merely foolish or downright dangerous? Would we think of these people as rational? Would rational people sabotage their own well-being, their own possibilities for the future? What would be the point of such behavior? What in the world could they be thinking?

What are we thinking when we invest months of effort in our recovery only to let it dribble away? If the meetings are working for us, is it rational to stop going? If we've suffered for want of love, isn't it self-defeating to stop phoning our new friends in the fellowship? Aren't we sabotaging our own possibilities when we get more interested in the lives of TV characters than we are in our own lives? We don't have to be insane to be self-saboteurs — we just have to stop thinking.

I will be on guard against complacency and laziness. I refuse to jeopardize my own progress.

December

*God gave us a memory that we might
have roses in December.*
— *James M. Barrie*

Feelings come to have many meanings for us.
Not a few of those meanings are negative. We
come to fear a great many things, but feelings can
also work as markers in time which help us clear a
path back to the experience that generated the feeling. A nasty burn, for example, with its accompanying feelings of pain and panic, reminds us of
that event. And those feelings certainly form our
thinking about fire.

The same thing happens every time we feel
peace, joy, success, and happiness. That's why it's
so important that we play, even if it feels uncomfortable; that we celebrate, even if we feel undeserving; that we laugh, even if we don't think we
know how.

Each time we do those happy things, those recovery things, we plant a marker that makes it
easier for us to find our way back to that happy
state and to experience that feeling again.

*What I can do once, I can do twice. I'm learning
that feelings can help as well as hurt me.*

December 2

Worry is a state of mind based on fear.
— *Napoleon Hill*

A major task of recovery is renaming many of the self-defeating, possibly neurotic, patterns we've learned to call by other names. Those of us who live under a cloud of worry, for example, never call it that — we simply say that we are fine.

It isn't hard to justify any self-defeating pattern that finds a home in our hearts and heads. We simply put a better face on it and rename it. Worry, however, is an expression of fear — fear of being happy, fear of succeeding, fear of breaking the old rules that life is a grind and happiness is unrealistic. Unless we take a good look at our lives, we accept these ideas as rules, and we obey them.

In the light of reason we often come to see that some of the "rules" we follow don't make any sense. We come to recognize the fear in the background, but we also recognize that the fear has no foundation in objective fact. At that point we are free to make a decision about what path we shall choose.

Fear is the companion of the isolated. I am not alone now, and I am not afraid.

*How does discretion fit in with open-
ness? I worry about careless talk.*
— *Vonnie W.*

All information isn't meant to be shared — other
people's confidences, for example, or tidbits of
gossip that are just as likely to be untrue as true.
Nor is it prudent to broadcast all the details of our
private lives, either in public or in meetings of
adult children. Especially when our stories involve
intimate details about friends and family members.

Personal revelation is important to recovery, but
where do we draw the line? Sharing is magic, and
the secrets we refuse to share can weigh down our
wings. What is appropriate?

Two guidelines have helped other recovering
people: *Find a trusted sponsor.* We can rely on our
sponsor's judgment, as our own develops, to determine which items are safe for group discussion and
which aren't. *When in doubt, don't.* If there's any
question at all about breaching someone else's pri-
vacy, we should say nothing until we've carefully
thought through the consequences. We can always
speak out at a later time.

*Today, I pray for the wisdom to share what I
should and leave the rest unsaid.*

December 4

It is good to act as if. It is even better to grow to the point where it is no longer an act.

— *Charles Holton*

Many of us do not even know what feeling jolly is like, let alone *being* jolly because of a calendar date. As much as we'd like to rise to this puzzling condition, the fact that the holidays are coming only makes us feel guilty somehow.

It doesn't help to be told we should be merry and lighthearted at this time of year. But it does help to remind ourselves that holiday celebration is largely a matter of choice. We can choose to join the flow of holiday shoppers and buy gifts for the people we love. We can choose to smile, to enjoy the music, cook special foods, and have friends in.

Heaven knows we've had some experience at faking our feelings. We can do so again. And who knows — maybe this time we'll get caught up in it instead of "acting as if."

Today, I ask God for the grace of a glad heart.

*To live means sharing one another's
space, dreams, sorrows, contributing
our ears to hear, our eyes to see, our
arms to hold, our hearts to love.*
                              — Paul Tillich

Effective, creative living takes practice and work. It's important to understand that. Like learning to run a household or manage a company, learning to live happily and well is a matter of acquiring skills. How skillful we are is almost always in direct relationship to how much we practice. "Once in a while" doesn't get it.

Think of it as a tug-of-war between who we are right now and who we want to be: One pulls hard; the other pulls harder. Who will win? Who we are now is strong with programmed response, learned reaction, and comfortable, customary, emotional patterns. We are the sum of what we were. And the past is powerful. Our new, becoming self, the self we want to be, is young and without the strength of personal history. How will that self gain power if exercised only once in a while?

The hours and days of our lives can grow increasingly brighter through all our remaining years if the self we are becoming is willing to pump enough iron.

Today, I will congratulate myself for the strength and insight I have worked hard to acquire.

December 6

> *I always feel better when I've been with my friend.*
>
> — *Charlotte Y.*

Some people lift our hearts in a very special way. Maybe it is their tenderness, their humor, or their ability to listen attentively that attracts us. Our friendships may be based on many things — hobbies, jobs, community involvement, or any other activities that draw like-minded people together. Within our closest friendships, we probably find that the best of us and of our friends comes together.

Friendships have a positive effect on self-esteem because they allow us to mirror back what we most appreciate in each other. This appreciation is not based on artificial encouragement, but rather on an honest reflection of the strengths of the friend. No wonder we feel so good when we're with our friends; they show us the best of what we are and encourage us to continue growth in positive directions. These healthy relationships allow us to move steadily away from the people-pleasing we once practiced. They give us a clear reflection of ourselves as joyful and lovable people.

Today, I will be aware of the healthy qualities I reflect to my friends.

*Let us run with patience the race that is
set before us.*

— Hebrews 12:1

We often find newcomers to adult children
groups exhibiting impatience with their growth.
The comments are similar to "Why is this taking so
long," "I must be doing it wrong because I don't
seem to be making any progress," or "Why are they
improving more than I am?"

There is no competition in recovery. The wise
response to such comments is "Tell me, how long
have you been practicing the habits and patterns
that got you here?" The answer of course is "All
my life." The obvious response to that is "Then
why do you think a few weeks or months is sufficient to turn that lifetime of habit around? Be patient."

We must learn to be much more patient with life
and, most of all, patient with ourselves.

*I am learning to be satisfied with progress rather
than perfection.*

December 8

Never let yesterday use up today.
— Richard H. Nelson

Boundaries are the issue. How often we talk about boundaries. Most often these are boundaries between us and other people. Where does my responsibility end and yours start? But there are other boundaries — mental boundaries. One of them is getting lost in yesterday.

Yesterday's fears can overrun the boundary of today like cattle through a broken fence. We can lose sight of the difference between what happened yesterday and what can happen today. We can allow yesterday's resentments to become today's facts or yesterday's expectations to become today's prophecies. Yesterday's people may become the people we deal with today. Our fathers become our husbands or male friends. Patterns between our mothers and their family systems become the expected norm for today. It is unfair to do this to those around us now.

Today is like a bright, new coin. It is potential, waiting for us to decide what we shall spend it on. We have a choice, as always: yesterday's hurt or today's celebration.

Today's possibilities need not be limited by the past. I choose to be happy and healthy for this 24 hours.

Success is to be measured not so much by the position that one has reached in life as by the obstacles which he has overcome while trying to succeed.
— *Booker T. Washington*

Competition can be a killer. Allowing our value or worth to be measured against the achievements of another leads to confusion and a misunderstanding of the truth.

We are not all the same. We have not all started at the same place. The effort and heroism it has taken to reach a certain level of success, on whatever field it may be played, vary as greatly as the players in this game of life.

Our task is to learn to stay within ourselves. We must learn to measure our grandness, not by another's yardstick or in relationship to another, but to know ourselves well enough to acknowledge the effort and desire we have put forth to get where we are — wherever that may be.

Today, I will not worry about who's ahead or who's behind. I will run my own race.

December 10

> *Many times our lives are scattered in-*
> *stead of centered.*
>
> — *Rich H.*

Whatever is not focused tends toward emotional diffusion. Many lives, scattered like leaves in the wind, are spent first dealing with one issue, then another, then yet a third. Nothing is focused; nothing ever finished.

Healthy living demands enough of a central focus that something gets finished once it gets started. Lacking this we often return to fight the same battle once again.

Recovery demands not that we heal every wound immediately, nor that we battle a dozen fronts at once, but that patiently, sanely, we pick one area, start someplace. We can spend a major portion of our lives waiting to discover just the right place to start. It is as if when we find that magical, totally clear issue to begin dealing with, then everything will fall into place and recovery will become easy.

Once we start, any place, we find that all issues are connected, and a bright window in any area of the house brightens the whole.

A focused sense of purpose is my goal for today.

*Any man can seek revenge, it takes a
king or prince to grant a pardon.*
— *Arthur J. Rehrat*

Revenge is the simplest and easiest of quests. But
it is a self-defeating action. It doesn't get the job
done.

Forgiveness, on the other hand, is the gesture of
a healthier mentality and power. The nobility of
pardon is in the elevated wisdom that by not forgiving we are, in fact, injuring ourselves. As long
as we fail to forgive we condemn ourselves to be
fixated at our point of pain.

Carrying our anger, rage, and revenge from the
past into the present can become an automatic response. We will probably need to work overtime
to maintain and justify our outrage at what happened to us in the past, and at the price we have
paid since. We can become so single-minded that it
becomes a holy mission to carry this blind resentment to the grave.

But then we become like a grave, and the lack of
pardon is the corpse within, contaminating everything we touch.

*As I grow in understanding, I grow in forgiveness.
Today, I will practice my program and continue to
grow.*

December 12

*Tell me what company you keep, and
I'll tell you who you are.*

— *Cervantes*

Program lore frequently reminds recovering
people to beware of slippery people and slippery
places. The obvious fact is, if we hang around
slippery people and places, we will slip.

Adult children are on slippery ground when
they try to communicate with people who constantly feel negative about life or negative toward
them specifically. Many adult children find the
most slippery place on earth is returning to their
original families. Many have to make very conscious decisions about how safe it is for them to
return home. Our whole task is to grow in the
realm of self-esteem and self-confidence. This demands that we experience some success. If we are
surrounded by those who only tell us what cannot
be done or what we cannot accomplish, we are
headed for a slip.

"Stick with winners," we are told. Stick with
those people who help push us up the hill — not
those who drag us down.

*I am not obliged to spend my life with people who
diminish my life. My choice of company is mine.*

*If you dam a river it stagnates. Running
water is beautiful water. So be a chan-
nel.*

— *English Proverb*

Pain has a loud voice. When we are in distress
our attention and energies naturally turn inward.
When we are wounded and bleeding we don't care
about concerns as mundane as the price of gas.

It is as it should be.

Yet at some point, the intense inward look is no
longer necessary and can actually be counterpro-
ductive. At that point we need to look beyond
ourselves and be willing to aid in the healing of
others.

An all-too-quick adult child's shame-based response is "But I have nothing to give. I can barely
keep my own nose above water." Such is not the
case.

Most adult children have suffered. We can share
that. We can have enormous encouragement and
understanding as a gift to heal others. To the degree that we have learned to work through our
own pain and to exhibit a sense of our own power,
we can show others that none of us has to be a
victim of the past.

God loves and accepts me as I am — and so do I.

December 14

Health and cheerfulness mutually beget each other.

— *Joseph Addison*

Promoting our own physical well-being is as much a part of recovery as reprogramming our past. We live in our bodies, after all, and the condition of those bodies either limits or expands our capacity for emotional management, our ability to concentrate, and the amount of patience we are able to bring to bear on our lives.

How much energy do we have? Many people say that the energy they have to spend is directly proportionate to the amount of exercise they get during the day. How much exercise do we get? The trick as always is not to bound into some unrealistic, overdemanding exercise program. We need not go into debt acquiring the latest equipment or joining the latest fad club. It may all start with a simple commitment to walk around the block.

The fact is we aren't mind or spirit or body; we are all of them acting together, intermingling, affecting one another. To abuse any part of who we are limits the totality of who we can be.

Today, I will eat nutritious foods and get some exercise.

Great works are performed not by strength but by perseverance.
— *Samuel Johnson*

Sometimes a relationship needs closure because it has run its course. Although we may have been involved for a long time or even be dependent on this person or relationship, we know it must end. For our sake. For that person's sake. For recovery's sake.

The temptation to waffle can be enormous: We can claim closure and still see the other person. We can declare closure and still read old love letters, drive around the other's house, frequent all the places "we" used to visit.

As understandable as these behaviors are and as deep as the panic and pain of closure may be, none of these behaviors accomplishes closure. To keep the door open even a crack means there is no closure. Closure means *closed.* Closure means dead.

If there is no closure on the past, there is no openness to the future. The pain may be fierce at first, but if closure is called for, closure must be served.

Today, I put my fear of separations and endings in the hands of my Higher Power.

December 16

All the mighty world of eye, and ear,
both what they half create, and what
they perceive.
— *William Wordsworth*

On a morning television show there was a segment on pets. People brought their favorite pets. One pet was a hairless cat — curious to be sure but by most standards not beautiful. The host cautiously asked, "But isn't it ugly?" The somewhat offended pet owner remarked, "Beauty is in the eye of the beholder!"

Perception is largely what forms our lives. Life truly is created by not only what we see and feel, but also how we see and feel. What is a catastrophic failure to one, is an opportunity to learn to another. What is perceived as God picking on them to some people, is God assisting them to be strong to others. What is a failed childhood to one person, is a college of survival skills to another — where all graduates have Ph.D.'s.

It is not what happens or happened to us that matters, but how we view those happenings.

I am responsible for my own perceptions of the world. I accept the fact that the world I see is largely the world I make.

*An optimist expects his dreams to come
true; a pessimist expects his nightmares
to.*

— *Laurence J. Peter*

Sometimes the only thing we can change is our
attitude — and that is enough. Our attitude can be
much more important than the objective reality of
the situation.

One person who's stuck in traffic, fumes at fate,
snarling, "Why does this always happen to me?"
Meanwhile, the person in the car just behind,
stuck in the same impasse, sees the first person's
"lost" time as "found" time — the perfect opportunity to study a new language, meditate, or think
through a problem without the interruption of a
telephone call or visitors. One person sees only a
problem and responds accordingly; the other sees
an opportunity and likewise acts accordingly. The
traffic jam is the same for both of them, but their
attitudes about it are different — as are their blood
pressures.

Some see the past as a cruel sentence of doom
dispensed by an avenging God. Others see it as an
opportunity, fairly given or not, to build strength
and gain wisdom with the help of a loving God.
The difference is all in the attitude.

*I am learning to make the most of my opportuni-
ties.*

December 18

Perhaps I am stronger than I think.
— Thomas Merton

Self-esteem is based on our perception of our worth. That perception is largely based on our experiences. That is, as we perform — as our life happens — our experiences determine what our identity is. It is our perception of that identity that establishes our self-esteem and its counterpart, self-confidence.

Experience has often taught adult children they are powerless victims. All too often our experience is of having no strength to control the events around us. Fear, shame, abandonment become as much a part of our lives as play, safety, and encouragement are parts of others' lives.

When recovery begins, we do indeed learn that we have more strength than we thought, for as we recover, the experiences we engage in become more positive, more controlled. As opposed to the messages of old, we learn we are worthy, able individuals; we learn to expect success.

I am stronger and more able than I ever thought I was. Tomorrow I will be stronger than I am today.

All are architects of fate, working in
these walls of time.
  — *Henry Wadsworth Longfellow*

We indeed do make a difference. We have a choice of being the "salt of the earth" and a light on a mountaintop, or we can choose to be quite something else.

When we become agents of hurt to others it is more often a result of inattention than malice. Consider four ways we injure those around us. These patterns may have been formed long ago and be so normal we scarcely see the havoc they create.

CRITICIZING: It is neither our responsibility nor our privilege to barrage others with our judgments, accurate or not.

INSULTING: Snide comments, no matter how clever, rob people of their dignity and, over time, damage their sense of worth.

NAME-CALLING: Calling people disparaging names, even if we're only "kidding," is a form of abuse.

IGNORING: Indifference is cruel; neglect is an insult. People who have been ignored have serious doubts about their value, if not their very right to exist.

Today, I will recognize the powerful effect my bad habits can have on other people. I will resolve to learn other ways.

December 20

Whatever is only almost true
is quite false
And among the most dangerous
of errors.
— *Henry Ward Beecher*

What is called "cash register honesty" is not usually a problem for adult children. We probably don't cheat people or steal their money, and we're probably not pathological liars. But many of us do have a problem with honesty, just the same. Self-honesty is what trips us up.

Honesty is both the benefit and the burden of recovery. Half-truths and unacknowledged truths are the root cause of most of the tangled, conflicting situations we find ourselves in. What we thought, we never clearly stated; what we needed, we never frankly asked for; what we intended to do, we never unmistakably declared. Our half-truths and double messages are the furthest thing from straightforward communication.

If we're honest with ourselves, we don't have to worry about being honest with other people. A self-honest person cannot tolerate duplicity. It's amazing how much simpler life is for self-honest people.

Straight talk is a result of straight thinking. I am
growing more able to do both.

To say I am made in the image of God
is to say that love is the reason for my
existence, for God is love.
                    — Thomas a Kempis

Two deep emotional needs of every living human being are acceptance and love (to love and be loved). We need to know that the people we value find meaning in us.

The fact is we are all made for love. Our hearts yearn for the locking connectedness that love entails. It is not just the feeling of love or being loved, but the actual connectedness that matters. We simply were not made to live alone.

We can find this connectedness in many places. For some, this basic need will lead to primary committed relationships. For others, it will be mainly satisfied by a deep family life. For yet others, it will take the form of "foster families" or deep friendships or working as volunteers with people who need us. We want to be with others. We want to love and belong.

And some, on the bottom line of their existence, through all the human manifestations of this need, find that all reaching for love is a reaching out for God. God as they understand God to be. God who is love.

I belong. I have a place. I love and am loved.

December 22

*I never trusted anyone. Then I learned
to trust myself a little bit. Then I
learned to trust God.*

— *Hank H.*

Saying that adult children have a trust problem
is like remarking that the Pope is Catholic. And we
all know why. To a greater or lesser degree, we all
put our bucket down the same dry well. When it
came up empty once too often, we decided trust
was a bad idea.

Our friends in the program have taught us differently. Now we realize that the real problem for
us is we weren't taught to be trustworthy. We're
not sure, you might say, what trustworthy looks
like. Reliability, loyalty, stability — are those the
key ingredients? Are we breaking trust when we
disagree or form an opinion of our own? Do we
have to be as predictable as the sunrise — every
day, every day, every day?

No, we don't have to be robots to be trustworthy. We have to learn to count on ourselves. Then
we won't have to wonder what trustworthy means.
We'll know.

*Today, I will seek to trust myself more. Today, I
will find small answers, not look at big questions.*

Some people walk in the rain. Others just get wet.

— Roger Miller

What does it mean to celebrate? To have a party? To get away? To buy ourselves something nice? To many of us it has meant, "Let's function less consciously. Let's turn on. Let's escape reality." Some versions are worse than others, but all of the above are imitations of celebration.

Authentic celebration is not so much escaping as it is coming back, not so much a lessening of consciousness as it is a heightening of consciousness. To celebrate is to re-create, refresh, and remake the spirit. It is to grow rather than to go or get or grab. How much happier our lives will be when we can say, "Come celebrate — let's talk. Come celebrate — let's walk in the park. Come celebrate — let's listen to the wind and watch the night fall. Come celebrate — let's dispel loneliness, get a sourpuss to smile, share ourselves with each other."

Today, I will rethink my old ideas about celebration. I will learn to lift up my heart in new ways.

December 24

Every Christmas I hope for the best but expect the worst.
  — Adult child group member

As bells ring out and carols echo everywhere, we should not be surprised if our spirits take a nosedive. It isn't that we don't understand the meaning of Christmas, or that we reject it, but rather that the idealized version of what Christmas should be has oftentimes been denied us. We may come to resent the fact that all this good cheer seems to be for other people, not us.

Our experiences may have had little to do with family togetherness around a glowing fireplace, loving conversation, and delighted laughter. Such scenes feel like an affront if there has been no family closeness, perhaps no gifts, and little or no overt love. Of course it's wrenching when our own experience clashes so painfully with advertised reality!

But every day is a chance for new experience. We can choose today to create the good cheer that wasn't created for us. It's too late to change yesterday's disappointment, but, if we choose, we can make this holiday season the one we'll remember.

I have made a conscious decision to leave past Christmases in the past. Today, I will begin to plan a celebration.

The art of progress is to preserve order amid change and to preserve change amid order.
— *Alfred North Whitehead*

All life is leave-taking. Life is process, and we are inevitably caught up in its flow. Our life is one long passage from one state, one condition, to another. Let's not be too serious about where we are at any given moment; soon we will be at another place. This is especially true when considering recovery. Recovery is a process, not a competition with ourselves or anyone else. We never will be "there" because our capacity to grow is too great for that.

Many of us thought childhood would never end. It did. Then we thought we would never be anything but adolescents. We passed through that state as well. Perhaps we can no longer remember a time when we were not married, but that time did exist. Perhaps we never thought there would be a time when we were not married, but that may have happened also.

Like a leaf in a stream, we are on the move. It's silly to get too attached to any particular point of the journey.

I now hold my life tenderly and with open hands. I no longer think of all change as negative.

December 26

There is no such thing as something for nothing.

— *Napolean Hill*

We have often heard "If it sounds too good it probably is." Whether we know or accept that or not, it is a tantalizing temptation to expect — or at least hope — that we will find a free ride. Or at least cut-rate.

But all truly worthwhile things in life require full measure of effort and diligence. That which is not directed and tended will invariably go astray. Personal growth is no exception.

If we are to battle out of the self-defeating patterns generated by adult children environments, we must be willing to practice at least as hard at recovery as we practiced rooting the habits in our lives that cause us distress. How often did we practice those defeating ways of thinking, acting, feeling? Every day. Many times a day!

Even though there is no such thing as something for nothing, we can thankfully pay the price of recovery a small bit at a time.

I am willing to do a day's work for a day's progress. I know I can expect no more.

Having had a spiritual awakening as the result of these steps, we tried to carry this message to alcoholics, and to practice these principles in all our affairs.

— *Step Twelve of*
Alcoholics Anonymous

It has often been said that the only thing you can get more of by giving it away is love. Step Twelve advises us, out of loving hearts and grateful spirits, to "grow" our love by sharing it.

Countless others are suffering just as much and feeling just as lost as we did before we found the program. No doubt they, just as we did, have just about given up looking for the answers and the support they so desperately need. Perhaps they are on the brink of despair.

In Step Twelve, we throw open the doors of the banquet hall to those who are still standing outside in the cold. We welcome them as we were welcomed. We offer them our experience, strength, and hope.

I feel privileged to carry a message of understanding and hope to any brother or sister who will listen.

December 28

I couldn't hit a wall with a sixgun, but I can twirl one. It looks good.
— *John Wayne*

Many of us adult children fake emotions because our past experiences never taught us how to use boundaries when dealing with feelings. Now we are oftentimes stumped when it comes to knowing how we should feel or act when we are faced with emotional situations.

Sometimes we need to learn to "fake it till we make it"; what is asked of us is to act the part until the part becomes us.

We may not know how to feel anticipation around holidays — but we want to experience joy. We may not know what it feels like to really trust someone, but we would love to be in that position. What we can learn to do is "act as if" — working all the time to liberate the frozen emotions of years gone by — until we actually do experience what we seek.

Like new shoes, my new behaviors and feelings will feel stiff and uncomfortable for a little while. I am willing to live through the "breaking in" period.

Judge not, that ye be not judged.
— *Matthew 7:1*

Many adult children have found insight as well as freedom by working through what is called Family of Origin work. That is taking a detailed look into the past to understand its effects upon us.

At times, while working through this process, we tend to generate considerable anger and resentment toward our parents. Once some patterns and issues are seen, the temptation may be great to blame them for all our present ills and wounds.

Consider five, ten, or fifteen years from now. Your children will be in the process of working through their family of origin. Your life with them now is their family of origin in the future. Such reflection has enormous power to diffuse our own resentment.

Are we not trying as hard as we can now? Are we not playing with the best cards we have now? No matter how inadequate or what mistakes we may make — are we not doing all we can?

Didn't those who went before us do the same?

I am learning to let go of blame as I discover my own need for mercy.

> *The hero is no braver than the ordinary man, but he is brave five minutes longer.*
> — *Ralph Waldo Emerson*

The word *hero* takes on a new meaning in the lexicon of recovery. Ordinarily, we use the word to describe someone who accomplishes an amazing feat under dramatic circumstances. Rescuing someone from injury, single-handedly charging a machine-gun nest — that's the sort of thing we usually call heroic.

The heroism of recovering people is not as glamorous or obvious. The daring deed may simply be continuing to try when all previous efforts have failed. It may be coming back to group again and again in spite of our fears. Those who tell the truth, no matter what it costs them, are surely heroes, as are those who, from the depths of their hearts, forgive a grievous wrong done them in the past.

All of us are capable of such heroic acts, and those of us who perform such acts of heroism have simply tried a little longer.

I pray for faith in the future and for the strength to carry on when I am tired and discouraged.

*Happiness comes of the capacity to feel
deeply, to enjoy simply, to think freely,
to risk life, to be needed.*
— *Storm Jameson*

The elusive butterfly of happiness has been
chased by humanity since the beginning of time.
Sages have said that happiness is indeed like a butterfly — try to catch it and it flees; sit quietly and
it will light on your shoulder.

Who are the happiest people we know? Those
who are fully human, which means they are able
and willing to feel, to celebrate, to challenge old
boundaries, to risk, and to allow others to need
them.

All of these abilities are directly attacked in dysfunctional homes. Adult children learn not to feel,
not to risk, not to think creatively. Our energies
were needed to protect ourselves from the very
experiences that are necessary for happiness.

The good news is that we have the power to
change. We can be like butterflies ourselves, but
we've got to leave the cocoon behind if we want to
fly.

*I know that I can't pull back from and reach out to
life at the same time. Today, I choose to reach out.*

INDEX